Aunt Pat.

Enjoy!

Rob Goodwin

PORCH SWINGS
AND
PRAYER

ROB GOODWIN

Inspiring Voices®

Author photo by -Sherry Johnson Morgan

Inspiring Voices books may be ordered through booksellers or by contacting:

Inspiring Voices
1663 Liberty Drive
Bloomington, IN 47403
www.inspiringvoices.com
1 (866) 697-5313

ISBN: 978-1-4624-1111-5 (sc)
ISBN: 978-1-4624-1112-2 (e)

Library of Congress Control Number: 2015902072

Printed in the United States of America.

Inspiring Voices rev. date: 02/12/2015

For Sherry Johnson Morgan, forever my
biggest fan and most loving friend.

For Paul and all that you do to encourage my dreams.

For my mother and her determined commitment
to provide the best for her children.

For the love of my life, for my Bertie Mae.

PROLOGUE

Granny used to say that if people were talking about you then it probably meant you were doing something really good or really bad, but *you* had to be the judge of that. "If you are doing what you want to do, Sugar," she'd call me, "then it matters not what the other fella has to say about it." So, when a lady from church told me that I should not visit the Ohatchee Church of Christ because they were up to no good, I decided to give them the benefit of the doubt. Within hours of submitting my email to the Preacher, Wayne Dunaway, via the church website, I had a response from him offering to meet me for a Coke.

I had fallen away from my first love, the Church. My battle with depression stole my joy and drove a wedge between The Lord and I. Taking a job located hours away from family and living like a recluse made it easier for me to abandon the assembly. I offered every excuse in the book as to why I couldn't find a church home. My depression caused me to become weak in my faith and it nearly cost me my life.

Wayne Dunaway is a dear family friend. My grandmother on my Stepdad's side of the family had gone to church with him for many years. She and my Paw Paw Goodwin were actually founding members of the Ohatchee congregation. Brother Wayne preached Maw Maw Ruth's funeral. Even though I had known him for years, sitting down with him one on one in the summer of 2006 was a first. It also was a great turning point in life for me. It began a recovery from a very self-destructive cycle that lasted several years. I honestly never thought I would return to the Church of Christ. I was raised in a congregation with extreme legalistic views and in the back of mind I always wondered if I would ever have a hope of salvation, especially with my sins and mental turmoil.

Wayne is a man of God who preaches the Word. He also believes in emphasizing grace and mercy. What? Grace and mercy? Yes of course these are two very popular words in Christianity, but in a fire and brimstone culture, you don't hear much about them. Through several conversations and worship services with Wayne, I began to feel that I was definitely covered by the blood of Jesus and that it was something that had happened the moment I became born again. Previously, salvation was something I longed for or anticipated, but wasn't sure I deserved. At the Ohatchee Church, I learned that I had already received it. It was a done deal as long as my heart remained right with God. As long as I stayed a believer, I was okay.

Once Brother Wayne learned some of the talents I possessed and the nature of my last manic episode as a Bipolar, he insisted that I utilize the gift of public speaking to share my experiences. I had never considered speaking publicy about suicide attempts, alcohol binges, or other destructive behavior associated with my Depression. As a young boy, I remembered a lady being "dis-fellowshipped" or ex-communicated from The Church for simply taking Prozac. Wayne continued to encourage me and he convinced me that by speaking out, I could open the eyes of many about a very sensitive but prevalent issue among Christians.

In the spring of 2007 I stood before some 200 members of our church, family, and friends to share my message. I talked about the beautiful mountains overlooking the Calhoun County area of Alabama where we had all grown up. Cheaha Mountain is known as the highest point in the state of Alabama. Mt. Cheaha towers over the region at 2,411 feet. Although it is no Mt. Ranier, Rushmore or Kilimanjaro, Cheaha is beautifully intimidating. My buddy Chris and I took up mountain biking and were training on some of the smaller trails in nearby White Plains. Eventually we hoped to bike with the pros at Cheaha. My maternal grandmother, Granny as I called her, suddenly passed away and I was quietly dying inside. I felt that I couldn't continue through life without her, so Cheaha would be the perfect place for a biking accident. As I reflect now, I can't believe that I was so strategic in "training for suicide."

As I stood in the pulpit and shared these feelings and thoughts with both loved ones and perfect strangers for the first time, I realized what God was calling me to do. I was not successful in taking my own life on Mt. Cheaha. There was a divine intervention and it was strong enough to shock me into recovery. Oh sure, I would fall again, several times, and will for the rest of my life, but from this episode I learned a great deal about myself and my disease.

As I concluded the sermon and offered the invitation to come forward for prayer I felt an enormous peace sweep over my entire body. When people say they have a weight lifted from their shoulders, I know exactly what they mean. I was light as a feather. God gave me a forum to unload my greatest weakness and sin. It was one of the most liberating experiences of my life. I was greeted with so much love, acceptance, and encouragement from this congregation on this day and many days to come. I am moved by the experiences people have shared about their struggles in the following days and weeks. We were all ashamed and thought by admitting we were depressed meant we were less than others or didn't deserve our salvation.

In the years ahead, I learned that it was necessary for me to reach as many people as possible and let them know that Depression and mental illnesses are real. They are just as serious as a broken bone or life threatening physical illness. Mental illnesses must be treated professionally. One cannot ignore Depression. There is no shame or weakness in publicly admitting your biggest struggles. Christianity is all about humbling ourself before the Lord and one another.

For thirty-seven years now I have struggled with Bipolar Disorder/Manic Depression. I have to stay on top of this illness just as much as my high blood pressure or any ailment a person might face. This book has been an enormous source of therapy. My deepest earthy love in this life was my maternal grandmother, Bertie Mae Cochran. In this book, I get to tell you our love story. I get to tell you how she influenced my life and many others. She flies high with the angels today and I know she is sitting in my cheering section in Heaven asking God to guide me safely home.

Bertie Mae could always be found cross-legged, apron tied around her waist, whistling and praying in her swing.

CHAPTER ONE

When I was a little boy growing up in rural northeast Alabama, the cotton mills were just a little more than two decades old. Cotton farmers who actually picked their own crops or hired day workers had changed over to large mechanical cotton pickers. Many kids who had grown up picking cotton in the Alabama fields were now full time employees of these textile mills. It was a better life for most and offered a consistent year 'round income for families.

My mother and her family farmed all along Alabama Highway 21 between Jacksonville and Piedmont in the 1940s and 1950s. Born to J.D. and Bertie Mae Cochran, Ona Lee was the middle daughter and fourth of six children. She was born in 1944 and gave birth to me at the age of 28 in 1972. By the time I was born, J.D. had succumbed to cancer, as did the youngest child, Luther. Bertie Mae, or Granny as she was to me, lived in a small trailer in our yard. She was my second parent, my best friend, my spiritual leader, and the sweetheart of my life. My mother and grandmother had already endured a lifetime of ups and downs by 1972. They always made me feel as though they were just waiting for me.

I guess you could say my mother Ona Lee was a trailblazer in the family. She was the first to become divorced. Granny didn't believe in divorce, because the Church of Christ and the Bible taught against it. My biological father, Bob Gowens decided to leave Mom and I for a "big fat woman from Piedmont." Our cotton-farming, cotton-milling family was brutally honest at times. They told it like it was. The big woman from Piedmont stole my Daddy, but from the stories I heard, there wasn't much theft. He was like a parked car with the windows rolled down and the keys in the ignition, ready to be stolen. As much as Granny didn't believe in divorce, she certainly didn't believe in remarriage, but Mom fell in love with Floyd Ray Goodwin and at the age of three, he became my stepdad. I called him Daddy for the rest of his life.

Bertie Mae didn't like it when her kids defied her, but she learned to adjust and love anyway. She was the most forgiving person I have ever met. She was strong-willed, yet so tender at the same time. Granny was the true matriarch of our blue collar Bama bunch. She knew the world was changing, but didn't believe she had to change with it.

Granny was a small woman with a hunch back from years of being stooped over in the cotton fields. They grew all of their own food, fetched water from the creek behind "the old home place" and slaughtered hogs. She kept her jet black hair slicked back and tied in a bun with twelve bobby pins securing it tightly on Sunday mornings for church. The rest of the week, she might only use six or eight pins. She kept an apron around her waste and never wore shoes. Her feet were conditioned for all four seasons of weather in Alabama. Granny wore thick glasses and soaked her teeth in Efferdent every night. She believed a spray can of Lintimist was necessary for all occasions. I loved everything about her.

Granny didn't drive, so she had to ride with us everywhere, but I heard stories that in the 1920's she had been behind the wheel of a T-Model and she often told me about taking a wagon to town when she was younger. Depending on others for transportation was not her choice, but cataracts were beginning to cover her eyes. Of course as her kids grew older and got jobs at the plants and mills, they could afford Chevy's, Mercury's, and Fords. As long as she got a ride to Church on Sunday and Wednesday she was fine. Her maiden name was Duncan and was quite influential in the Jacksonville Church of Christ, where she placed her membership. Deacons, Elders, Preachers, and Song Leaders were abundant on the Duncan side of her family. Marrying J.D. Cochran was difficult on her at times because J.D. didn't attend services and didn't insist his kids do so either. In his old age, Bertie Mae was able to wear him down, but a bout with the flu in the early 1960s kept him out one single Sunday. When the preacher came calling on Monday and found J.D. on a tractor, he chastised him about missing Sunday service. I don't know the whole story, but there's a tale of a preacher running top speed down Highway 21 with an old country guy hot on his trail on a tractor. J.D. never went back to service after that visit. Bertie Mae held her head high and continued. Both holding onto their pride and stern wills.

I was a sassy little boy. Even as young as five years old, I could get a little emotional and mouthy at times. Granny always solved the issue with a rolled-up newspaper, so I learned not to push my luck in her presence. For the most part, up until the year I started first grade at Roy Webb Elementary, I was a happy little guy. I had two Dads. My Daddy Bob didn't come around too much since Mom had re-remarried, so Floyd Ray was really Daddy to me. I fell in love with him immediately, just like my mother did. He was a handsome man and could fix everything. I remember how much he laughed and enjoyed having fun. He always had a smile and Daddy Bob always wore a frown.

Mom and Dad were expecting my new baby sister any day the year after my fifth birthday. Mom had been telling me that we were going to make some changes so that I could have the same last name as Dad, my new baby sister, my older stepbrother Tony, and of course her. I agreed that I wanted to be a Goodwin just like them. At the age of five I didn't want to be the only one in the house with a different last name. Bertie Mae did not approve of this at all. She felt from the beginning it was a bad idea. Even though I didn't see any of my real Dad's family except my Aunt Sylvia, or Aunt Wormy as I affectionately called her. Granny still thought that as I got older I would want to have a relationship with my Dad and his family. I liked the sound of the last name Goodwin. I wanted it to be my last name.

When Ona Lee married Floyd Ray I was standing right there beside them holding her hand. The Justice of The Peace asked that we close our eyes and pray. After the prayer he announced they were husband and wife. I announced that I was married too, because I closed my eyes also. Floyd Ray just ate that up. Yep, he was my Dad, too! I thought becoming a Goodwin sounded exactly like the right decision to make.

Daddy Bob came for a visit one afternoon and we delivered the news. Since starting school was right around the corner, Mom was taking the steps to change my name officially from Robby Gowens to Robby Goodwin. For some reason, Daddy Bob didn't take the news as well as I expected. He was devastated and angry. He and mother began yelling at each other. She reminded him that he had given up all rights when he requested the keys to their Nova and gave her the trailer and baby in exchange for not paying child support. I didn't understand adults at the age of five. I look back now and I am so angry that I was even in this situation.

Instead of pleading his case or simply objecting Daddy Bob turned to me. "I guess you really don't need me anymore, so you won't see me anymore," as he stormed out the door. I will never forget those words. He was blood red. What just happened, I must have been thinking? About ten seconds later I fell to the floor in tears screaming and rolling around as if I had been stung by a wasp. I don't think I really understood the brevity of what had just happened as we all heard the tires of the blue Chevy Nova squeal from the driveway. Mostly anger and sadness swayed back and forth in my mind as I ventured out on the front porch. I think I truly believed that he would turn around and come back. I honestly thought he was going to say to me that it was okay for me to take Daddy Floyd's last name. Boy was I naïve? No, I was just five years old and I didn't know any better and it was way too heavy of a subject for me to deal with at that age. It was traumatic.

I curled up like a Rolly Poly on the doorsteps and began sobbing harder. Arms swooped down and engulfed me and carried me away. It was Bertie Mae, my Granny. She knew it was coming and she was watching from across the yard. There was not anything she could do to prevent my pain. She was there to pick up the pieces. We made it to her porch and sat in the white wooden swing built for her by my uncle. I buried my face in her lap and cried as hard as I could. She prayed.

I am sure later she was able to reach my Daddy Bob on the phone and try and reason with him, but it never got better. I am sure she talked to my mother until she was blue in the face. I am sure she wanted to tell me "I told you so," when I was walking around for weeks before this day boasting about being a Goodwin. She never did though. She never made me feel like it was my fault. On this day, my first breakdown happened. I worried myself for weeks and months about what had happened. I became two different people in my mind, Robby Gowens and Robby Goodwin. I honestly feel like I split into two personalities from that point on and I became a very secretive child.

I wanted to be Floyd Ray's child. He had been my Daddy for over two years by now. I had a baby sister on the way and a big brother that I had come to love. Still, I ached for Daddy Bob. I never understood what went wrong in the marriage between my mother and Bob. They were married eight years before I was born. That was a long time. Mom always said Bob didn't want children; therefore I couldn't help but think I was the cause of the divorce. I think part of me believed that I was setting him free by changing my name.

Looking back, at the age of five, I wish I had not known all the details of my parents split. I wish my family had not told me of Daddy Bob's affairs. I wish I had not known that he was vocal about not having children. I wish I had done many things differently and I have obsessed over those wishes most of my life, contributing to many manic episodes.

The next year I began school at Roy Webb. My mother's sister Emily, her husband Thomas and their two daughters Rhonda and Sherry lived in the same yard with Granny and us. Rhonda and Sherry were like sisters to me as well. Emily was definitely another mother and Thomas another father figure. Our families were so close and I could always run to Emily or anyone in that family in tears and I often did. Sherry and I were the closest and still are today. We are only five months apart. She has been my protector my entire life. She has always known that I was the "weaker kid." I really don't know where I would be in life without that friendship. Rhonda was three years older than Sherry and I. She treated me as a baby brother also. Granny kept all of us kids while our parents worked in the mills and factories and we were able to form unbreakable bonds.

At Roy Webb, Sherry and I joined three more of our cousins in the same class. The class only had twenty-four total students. Our community was very small and close. Everyone knew everyone else. Our parents had great relationships with the teachers. My mother was a room mother every year at Roy Webb and never missed an event. She was extremely active in every aspect of my school days at Roy Webb. School was a great outlet for me. I met new friends, truly loved learning to read and write. At home I would continue school as much as possible constantly pretending and being creative.

In the first grade Valentines Day play, my best friend Sherilyn Johnson and I were cast as the Prince and Princess. Standing on the stage I remember looking out into the audience at my family with pride. I caught a glimpse of a very large man standing in the back of the auditorium and when our eyes met he slipped out the door. I had not seen Daddy Bob in over a year, but I could have sworn that was him. I wanted it to be him.

My baby sister Becky was literally my favorite toy next to a blank notebook and pencil. If I wasn't writing, then all of my attention was directed at her. I loved being a big brother. Since I was five years older than she, it was my job to teach her the ropes on everything and of course to mold her into the human being that I though she should be. Ha! Fortunately she had a mind of her own then and now and does a great job of taking care of herself.

Daddy Floyd and I just got closer after I took his name and I know that I should have been content with that. Dreams about Daddy Bob haunted me however and I think I never dealt with the damage appropriately. I can't blame anyone else either because in the 1970s there was not a lot of conversation about mental disorders, especially in children. My family just nicknamed me "The Worry Wart," and explained away all my erratic behavior with the fact that I worried too much about everyone and everything.

Bertie Mae has a total of fifteen grandchildren, but from the age of five I became her favorite and that is undisputed by anyone in our family. We were best friends. She saw what was happening to me and what I was becoming and I think she knew from that moment forward just how much I needed her. She would never let me down.

I often wonder what would life have been like if this family stayed together. Robby at age 2 with Bob and Ona Lee Gowens.

CHAPTER TWO

My bond with Bertie Mae continued to grow year after year of my young life. I found great comfort in her presence. The life lessons she taught each of her grandchildren will live on for many generations. My earliest memory of going to church with Granny is probably at the age of three or four. I enjoyed Sunday school at the Jacksonville Church of Christ and then snuggling next to Granny on the fourth pew from the front. My cousins, Rhonda, Sherry, Lee and Amy were always with us. Lee and Amy belonged to my mother's eldest sister, Myrtle and her husband Noble. Amy was the same age as Sherry and I, and Lee was about eight years older.

Sherry, my cousin is more like my twin. We have been inseparable since birth. It all started right there on Granny's doorsteps.

I took everything to heart that Granny told us. I hung on her every word. Bertie Mae was quite punctual in everything she did and so was my mother. I think it comes from working so hard as they were growing up. There was always so much to do and so little time to do it. My mother set a great example for me by always being ready for work very early and leaving in "plenty of time." Granny had the same attitude about Sunday school. Even though it was only a 15-minute drive from our home to the church building, we would leave a good 30 minutes before services began. Granny loved to socialize with her friends at the church.

My mother and her siblings did not attend church service when I was growing up. They always said they were made to go when they were younger and they were always tired from work or some other excuse they would give. However, Mom always insisted that I go with Granny and they knew how much worshiping The Lord meant to Granny. J.D. Cochran was a hard working and God fearing man, but he was not much for organized religion and each of his children shared that view. Bertie Mae and her family craved the weekly edification and believed it necessary to achieve Heaven's gates.

After learning to read in elementary school, I really enjoyed going to church service so much more. I would always raise my hand in Mrs. Betty Kelley's class to read the scriptures. Amy was a good reader as well, but of course I wanted to outdo her. Mrs. Kelley encouraged each of us to attend Sunday School each week, so she drew a cherry tree on the board for each student. Every Sunday that you made it to service, a new cherry was placed on your tree. If you were late (which I never was), you got a small black dot on one of your cherries. No one wanted a rotten cherry.

One summer I remember getting really ahead of Amy on the number of cherries on my tree. Amy missed two Sundays in a row and when she returned, Mrs. Kelley asked her, "Amy where have you been?" I will never forget Amy's candid reply, "sorry about that, we had to paint the porch and Mom said she didn't care whether you liked it or not." I nearly gasped when my outspoken little brunette cousin said those words to the ever-demure Mrs. Kelley. I could just see my Aunt Myrtle saying that. I could also see her tanning Amy's hide when she got back home for repeating that at church. Of course I had to tell Granny. I was quite the tattletale and I reckon it was frustrating for my cousins.

Sunday school ended at 10:15 AM and we would then return to the auditorium for regular worship service. At the Church of Christ this meant some old gentleman would stand up and welcome everyone. Regardless of who made the announcements, they all sounded the same. It was so robotic to me at that age. "Welcome to the Jacksonville Church of Christ, if you are visiting with us, please come back every opportunity. Members, take an attendance card from the pew in front of you, fill it out and pass it to the center aisle." Yes, I said fill out an attendance card! In the 1970s and 1980s they kept up with who attended and who did not. Tradition or unrealistic expectations, you decide?

Sherry, Amy and I took turns filling out the attendance card for Granny. We signed her name, Bertie Mae Cochran and then placed a comma with all of our names listed next. Granny shared her pew with a lovely little old lady named Pearl Dobbs. Pearl wore her hair in a large bun just like Granny except her hair was solid white. Granny always told us she had "Indian" in her blood and that is why her hair was jet black. She never colored it and it was completely natural, even into her nineties.

Pearl Dobbs was short and plump. She wore very floral dresses and usually had a belt tied just below her large bosom area. She also wore coke bottle glasses. They were so thick I never really knew what color her eyes were. After the welcome announcements and an opening prayer, my favorite part of the service would occur, the singing. At the Church of Christ we sing acappella. I enjoy singing without instruments because it enables you to hear all four parts; bass, tenor, alto, and soprano. We used gold songbooks or hymnals as they were called. Poor Ms. Pearl Dobbs couldn't see worth a flip even through her glasses, so I would sit in between her and Granny and find the songs for her when they called out a number. I would simply flip to the page in my book and then exchange with her. The next song, I would find it again and then we swapped books again. I enjoyed it and Granny said that was me doing The Lord's work. I liked that and it made me proud.

Pearl Dobbs loved on me often for helping her. Each Sunday as we were leaving the church we could see Pearl driving her 1957 Chevy from the parking lot. She would always be driving with her knees while she used a popsicle stick to place snuff from a can in her mouth. Granny would get onto her the next time we saw her. "Pearl you ain't got no business doing that, you are gonna get run over," Granny would say to her friend. Pearl replied, "she knows where she is going," referring to the red and white striped Chevy. I was sad when Pearl passed away, but Granny said she was nearly a hundred and I never realized that.

Bertie Mae had a lot of older friends from the church, community and of course extended family. I enjoyed just sitting and watching them talk. I would sit quietly and soak up everything they said. When someone would comment about how quiet I was or that I was just sitting there observing, Granny would always say, "he's gonna write a book one day," and just laugh. I am so glad she was right about that.

From everything I have observed over the years, it is pretty common for a grandmother to be like a second or third parent to her grandchildren. I am very close to my mother and was always a "Momma's Boy," and had a wonderful stepfather, but my relationship with Granny was extra special. She was my spiritual leader and as I reflect it occurs to me that she knew I was going to be very different than other kids. She recognized just how much I needed her and would need her for the rest of my life. I am so grateful for that bond and the unique attention and care that she gave me.

After Daddy Bob walked away I began to get in trouble for emotional outbursts. They would occur randomly and there is no wonder that my mother or anyone else couldn't understand what was going on. I was well taken care of, provided for with a seemingly happy life, but that is how Bipolar Disorder and Depression work. Mental illness is not easy to interpret, understand or predict. Mental illnesses are complex, contradictory, and debilitating.

One late summer day Mom and Daddy Floyd were both working second shift at Blue Mountain Cotton Mill in Anniston. Most of the time while I was growing up, they worked separate shifts, but occasionally overtime was available or some special reason they needed to work the same shift. Granny was always there to step in and take care of my little sister Becky and I. On this particular day Granny was in the back bedroom of our trailer changing Becky's diaper and I was wondering around in the kitchen, or "pilfering" as they would say. Mom made blueberry muffins the day before and I had enjoyed one earlier in the day. When I glanced to the counter beside our old brown refrigerator there was only one muffin left. I couldn't believe it. Mom and Dad would be home later and there would only be one muffin for them. I collapsed on the floor screaming and crying.

Through my screams I could hear and feel Granny running down the hall toward me. She reached down and picked me up, pulled out a kitchen chair and sat down where she could get a look at me. I was a puny and tiny six year old, so it was easy for any adult to physically handle me.

Granny ran her hands all through my hair, up and down my body, looking for some cut, scratch, bruise, bee sting…something to give her an indication of why I was screaming for bloody murder. She shook me, grabbed my face and blew air toward me. Finally I was able to form a couple of sentences and explain to her that there was not enough muffins for Mama and Daddy and they would have to fight over it when they got home and then he might leave. She was shocked and so was I when she grabbed her newspaper and swatted me. I scared her to death. She stood up and kind of stumbled holding on to the table. "Boy, what is wrong with you?" she asked. We both stood there in silence for a few moments and then she took me by the hand and led me back to where Becky was laying in the bed. We sat down and she asked me why I worried so much. I couldn't explain. I didn't know.

Even as a young child my mind raced out of control. I concocted horrible scenarios of tragedy. I was obsessed with losing loved ones and thinking people were going to walk away from me, die, or just disappear. I needed help, I clung to Granny and she did everything for me that she was capable of doing.

At night when my parents would come home from work or it would be just a normal bedtime, I always had to make a phone call to Granny to say goodnight. She might have just left our trailer for the short walk to hers, but I still had to call her and make sure she knew that I loved her. I would go to our old black rotary phone and dial 435-7566 each evening. She always knew it was me calling that time of the night and would answer "hello sugar." I would beg her not to die in the middle of the night and leave me. She always promised that she would be fine. I cried myself to sleep many times wondering if that would be my last day with my Granny. From our kitchen window I could see her trailer and her bedroom window. Some nights I would creep through the rooms to that window and watch to see if her light was on. If I was in really bad shape and couldn't go back to sleep I would dial her number, wait for the light to come on and then hang up really fast and scurry back to bed. Granny would tell my mother and aunts the next day that someone keeps calling her in the middle of the night and hanging up. I have no idea if they knew it was me. I regret interrupting her sleep, but it was the nature of my demon.

I felt genuine love for my grandmother as a young boy. I use the word obsessed at times because I couldn't let go of the worry about losing her some day. Looking back I think about all the happiness my worry and dread robbed me of. The sweet times could have been even sweeter if I were not struggling emotionally. It is very difficult to put into words the affects that a mental illness can have on your daily feelings. Only those who suffer really understand the unpredictability of this ailment. I think people like my Bertie Mae are a gift from God. The Lord uses them as a life raft for those of us who constantly feel that we are barely hanging on.

Certainly my days were filled with joy and happiness. I loved going to school with my friends, playing with my cousins, baby sister and my parents. Just like my adult cycles come from out of nowhere, I experienced that as a child and it is forever burned in my mind. Proper diagnosis is so difficult for any person, but especially a child. A child is not capable of explaining the way an adult can. I found a wonderful outlet in writing as a young fellow. The beauty of putting words on paper was soothing to me. It was like an art to write in cursive or put full sentences together. I credit Granny with initiating my love for reading and writing because her vision was so bad, she always had me read to her.

I started by reading simple books like Dr. Seuss or Curious George, but then as I grew and read more literature, I was as entertained by my grandmother's expressions as I was the actual story in the book. I learned to really appreciate good storytelling and knowing your audience. I began to pick out great books that I knew would make Granny laugh, cry, or want to comment. I practiced emphasizing the words more just to gain more reaction even though I had no idea what that was called, I just did it naturally. This helped me to gain a passion for public speaking as well as reading and writing.

Granny adored watching The Waltons on TV. She could really relate to Grandma Esther Walton. She was stern but so loving. Granny thought Ester Walton was a smart lady and had more sense than the crazy Baldwin Sisters, Mamie and Emily. I never heard my grandmother breathe a bad word about anyone and certainly she would never think of using profanity, but when The Waltons would start talking about "The Recipe" and Mamie or Emily Baldwin came on the scene, Granny would have a few choice words for their silliness, much like Grandma Walton.

Bertie Mae took her grandchildren to every worship service she could. She helped shape the people we would become.

CHAPTER THREE

Station wagons were a big thing in the 1970s in rural Alabama. The back door was perfect for loading and unloading groceries or other supplies and many wagons had a pop up third row seat that faced the rear. I have to chuckle a little about the psychology of the very back seat facing backwards. Just the other day I noticed a commercial for Volvo where a young lady was driving a new wagon. She was daydreaming about sitting in the back of her parents Volvo wagon and facing backwards. "Now, I only face forward," she quipped as she sped off in the Swedish wagon. I loved our station wagons and as a little boy, I used the back seat for writing. Whenever I got bored playing outside with my cousins, I'd just raise the back hatch, climb in with one of my notebooks and start writing short stories.

Jacksonville, AL is a great town. I loved growing up there and now that I am back home living in the same town, I just absolutely cherish it. Jacksonville has a wonderful state university, JSU (Jacksonville State University), which originally opened as a teaching college and later advanced to a full university. The population fluctuates 10K or more during the fall and spring and of course drops off during the summer. Ft. McClellan was a major military base just a few miles south of Jacksonville and remained open until the early 1990s. There was quite a mix of culture in our area growing up, due to the military families and their influence.

On Saturday mornings while my sister Becky and I watched Super Friends and Scooby Doo, Mom would tease her hair and get ready to go to town. Our little community of Roy Webb was only about eight miles outside the Jacksonville city limits, but in the country, that's a long way! We piled into the station wagon and ventured into town each Saturday to buy groceries. Occasionally my Aunt Emily, Rhonda and Sherry would join us, but many times we just went separately. Thomas and Emily decided to move into a brick home just across the hill from our trailer compound in 1978, but we still saw them almost daily. Granny moved into their larger single-wide trailer directly behind our 1964 Wolverine. Mom and Daddy Floyd built a couple of rooms onto our trailer so we had all the space we needed. I always daydreamed about a new home, but my parents did the best they could and they were both very content. My mother has never been a materialistic person. She got that from her parents. Ona Lee often refers to herself as "just plain folks" when she meets new people. She loved to entertain though. Regardless of the small size of our home, Ona Lee is known as quite the hostess. Her large pans of chicken and dressing, dumplings, friend green tomatoes and so much more have always been a huge hit with every branch of our family. Mom may not have ever been known for having the best home, but she has always had the best home-cooking!

At the end of our Saturday shopping sprees at the Super Value, Mom would drive down to the best hamburger joint in the world, The Rocket. This small rock shack sat on the edge of town just south of the square and university. The Rocket was a drive-in. As Mom pulled her station wagon into a stall, I would climb across two rows of seats and across her lap to reach out the window and grab the black phone receiver to place our order. I loved telephones back then and I still do now. Of course I have a smart phone, but if I could just hook a receiver to it, I would carry that around all the time. When I visit antique stores today, I love to look at old rotary dial phones. I like the tan ones and green ones. We always had a black phone and as a child I desperately wanted a tan rotary dial phone or a green one like they had in the Olan Mills Photography studio in Anniston. Phones were just another way to communicate, and I was fascinated.

One Saturday morning while visiting The Rocket I climbed across my mother's lap and got my leg caught in the steering wheel causing my mother to run into a pole at one of the stalls. It only bent the pole slightly, but it remained that way for more than a decade. Of course I cried like crazy when I caused "the wreck" but later I would appreciate that bent pole and look at it with honor. I did that, ha!

The crash into the pole caused the radiator to crack on Mom's wagon. She had to go inside and borrow the phone to call my Daddy Floyd. He came to pick us up in his Ford Grand Torino Station Wagon. It was green with wood-grain panels along each side and a luggage rack on top. The seats were a thick green vinyl and you could slide in one door and out the other quickly because they were so slick. My small behind would fit on the armrest of the passenger door. Dad would drive, Mom sat in the middle and I rode shotgun sitting up high on that tiny armrest looking out at the world.

On Sundays we drove the Gran Torino to Ohatchee, to the southwest of Jacksonville. Ohatchee was barely a town, mostly a community, but it did have a small city hall and a high school. The Goodwin family lived in Ohatchee and so we drove down to Boiling Springs Road each week to have dinner with Maw Maw and Paw Paw Goodwin. I still attended morning church service with Bertie Mae, but Mom and Dad would drive over and pick me up afterwards and we headed to Ohatchee. Floyd Wesley and Ruth Goodwin were my step-grandparents but never used the word "step" with me. They loved me as their own, just like my older stepbrother Tony and younger half-sister Becky. The Goodwins attended the Ohatchee Church of Christ, so they had a lot in common with Bertie Mae. In fact, Ruth and Bertie Mae became best friends. I have never seen two in-laws love each other more.

Maw Maw Goodwin was a robust little lady. She was about 4'10" and very busty with a small waist and large hips. She always explained her size by saying, "I had my stomach stretched seven times," referring to her offspring. My mother would cringe when she said that. Any pregnancy talk around the kids was taboo in that day and age. My mother was very prudish and conservative. She refuses to watch television today because of the "filth" and terrible language that is broadcast. I have to agree with her sometimes. Cable programming is nothing compared to the Happy Days, Laverne and Shirley or even Charlie's Angels type of programming I grew up watching.

Maw Maw dipped Brut snuff and Paw Paw smoked cigarettes. They had two rocking chairs on their tiny porch and that's where he would be seated when we pulled in the driveway. Paw Paw was a tall slim man with very thin hair. My mother and I thought he hung the moon. Ona Lee missed her father J.D., and never had a relationship with her first Father-in-Law so she truly bonded with Floyd Wesley Goodwin. Sometimes Mom doted on Paw Paw so much that it made Ruth jealous.

What a blessing it was for my Granny Cochran (Bertie Mae) and Maw Maw Goodwin (Ruth Mae) to become best friends. They both taught me so much and loved me more than anyone deserves.

The Goodwin family loved to gather and eat. My aunts, uncles, and cousins would all pour in after church services and spend the entire day. Mom and my grandmother cooked up a storm and we were all very well fed. Skinny pine trees were abundant in the yard adjacent to the house, so my cousins and I ran and played for hours. Every Sunday we were able to see my grandparents, Aunt Doris and Uncle Buck and my Dad's two younger sisters who were twins, Irma and Barbara. The twins were hilarious to me because they were constantly arguing about who was younger, prettier, etc. They finished each other's sentences and just seemed so sophisticated to me. In their younger days they worked in the cotton mills, but later progressed into professional careers in Insurance and Real Estate and I was in awe of them. I wanted to be just like them when I grew up. They all had beautiful homes. We were the only ones who lived in a trailer and I admired those relatives. I often daydreamed about having the homes they enjoyed.

Aunt Irma's husband, Doug Laney was one of my favorite uncles of all. I would crawl up in his lap and tell him "fairytales." I always started a story with the same opening, "Once aponce a time." I got a little confused and meant to say, "Once Upon A Time," but that was just my way and he would roar with laughter each time I made the faux pas. He nicknamed me, "Ponce-a-time" and I still wear it proudly today. I love and respect that man and adore my Aunt Irma. She has been a great friend in my life and they all made sure that I never felt like an outsider. They were so proud that I took the Goodwin name. I was incredibly blessed by this family and for a while it was easy for me to forget my biological family.

Toward the end of our Sunday visits, Paw Paw would be hinting to Mom and Dad when Maw Maw was not around that he was running low on cigarettes. I am sure they were on a fixed income and Maw Maw did not want her husband smoking, even though she enjoyed her Brut. Dad would load me and Paw Paw up and take us down to Kelley's store, buy him a carton of cigarettes and a half gallon of black walnut ice cream for Maw Maw. As long as we brought something back for my grandmother, she would let it go that Paw Paw asked for new cigarettes. Everyone would be happy and we all left with smiles on our faces. I would sit in the back of the station wagon as we left so that I could wave to them until we were out of sight, then I'd climb over all the seats and return to my vantage point on the armrest alongside Mom and Dad.

Traveling through communities like Alexandria and Cedar Springs on our way home, we passed a lot of houses. As the sun went down I could see in the windows of houses with their lights on. Bi-level and tri-level homes were popping up everywhere and I was fascinated by this architecture. I would turn my head and nearly give myself a whiplash trying to see inside a house and where their staircase might be. I was a dreamer. It wrecked my mother's nerves because she said Bob was always that way. She didn't understand why I had to be the same way. I am sure one of the reasons my mother and Daddy Bob did not make it is because they had different hopes and dreams in life. My mother finds ambition to be wasteful and Bob, he was a dreamer.

I enjoyed building my own house in our living room. This room was an addition to the trailer and it was large to me. I took boxes, blankets, and a plastic tunnel I had as a toy and constructed my own playhouse in the corner. I would sit in there for hours, talk to myself, read, write, and daydream. When things bothered me the most, that's where I would retreat. I remember one week in particular Paw Paw had been in the hospital shortly before I turned seven. We didn't see him that Sunday and they would not allow me to visit the hospital. I could tell Mom was sad and worried, so of course I was as well. I hid in my little playhouse and prayed the way Granny taught me. My aunt Emily walked through the door from our porch and grabbed my mother, "Irma called, Paw Paw just died." My Mom just collapsed in screams and I bolted from my hidden cave scaring the life out of both women. "Not my Paw Paw," I kept yelling. Mom gathered herself as best she could and Emily took her to the cotton mill to tell Daddy Floyd. Both my parents were startled because they didn't know he was that sick. Floyd Wesley Goodwin died at the age of 72 and he was the only grandfather I had the chance to meet and love.

Over the next few days and weeks I watched my Dad sit in silence and cry over losing his father. I felt that kind of love and compassion for my mother, but I just didn't understand someone being that upset over losing their father. For me there was a major difference in my relationship and love for my mother than for Daddy Floyd or Daddy Bob.

I have never really grasped the concept of a person loving both parents equally. I thought about Daddy Bob during this time and I remember wanting to call him and tell him about losing my Paw Paw Goodwin and thinking that he might be sad for me. Anything I experienced in life I wanted to tell Daddy Bob. I brainstormed as a child and embellished events so much trying to make him feel compassion for me. Daddy Floyd told me that when he stared out the window he felt as if Paw Paw was somewhere looking out as well and they were thinking the same things. I wondered if that worked for me and Daddy Bob, so I would stare off into space and imagine that he was somewhere doing the very same thing.

CHAPTER FOUR

I am in love with Roy Webb, the community. People talk about their hometowns being God's Country and I feel exactly the same about our little section of the world. The Roy Webb Road runs north of Jacksonville into a rural area of Piedmont known as Knightens Crossraods. Cotton fields, cornfields, and small country homes lined the road in the 70s. Roy Webb School sat atop a hill overlooking the road with its namesake. The school building was a solid brick structure. Two large entrances faced the roadway. Our five school buses lined perfectly along the gravel drive in front of the building. Several of the bus drivers were lunchroom ladies, so they parked the bus for the day. My bus driver, Robbie Williams returned home each day, but she was right back and sitting fourth in line every afternoon. I loved riding the bus and begged my mother to buy me five school buses to play with. I took a marker and wrote the numbers on them that matched our Roy Webb buses; 23, 144, 131, 86, and 109. I loved Mrs. Robbie and thought it was interesting that we shared the same name. Her son Jason was in my class and a very good friend.

The classes were very small at Roy Webb. The teachers and parents were on the same page. If a child got in trouble at school, the parents didn't go running up there the next day to jump on the teacher or Principal, the child got it worse when they got home. Mom always told me "if you get a paddling or sent out in the hall for something, when you get home I will whip you!" Teachers would call the parents of a misbehaving child if they needed to and that child would come to school the next day with a brand new attitude. That's how my generation was raised and I wonder where we went wrong with our kids? I never got a paddling the entire twelve years of my primary education because I feared what would happen at home. I wonder why parents have stopped supporting teachers and taking up for their children regardless of behavior. It's my generation that is responsible for the lack of respect today's youth have. We didn't raise our kids with a firm hand like our parents did. Is giving a child everything they want going to set them up for success or failure?

Our teachers took us to the playground in the afternoon to get physical exercise and to probably work out any mental pent up energy from being in the classroom all day. My friends and I ran and played hard. We had monkey bars, slides, and seesaws. Sherilyn Johnson and I formed a great bond from the first grade at Roy Webb on through adulthood. She was the prettiest girl in our class and all of the boys wanted to kiss her. I wanted her to be my sister. I loved everything about her. She wore her hair long and straight with pretty hair bows and always had a nice smile. She had an older sister, Missy who passed away before she was born, so Roy Webb kids were like siblings for Sherilynn. We sort of adopted each other. When I played school at home, Sherilyn was always in my class. She was one of my first role models.

A fall festival was held at the building each year to raise money. I loved it. We usually did a Halloween theme because it was held toward the end of October. In the gymnasium you could buy popcorn balls, cotton candy, and other snacks, play games and "go-fish" for prizes. Granny loved the Cake Walk and usually would win one for us each year. Downstairs, tucked away next to the lunchroom was the spook house. Mom was always resistant to let us go in because she thought we would have nightmares, but after older cousins assured her it was not that scary she would let us go. The spook house was my favorite part, I looked forward to it every year and yes it gave me nightmares.

Growing up in a small and close-knit community is an incredible blessing. I loved the first six years of school because Roy Webb was a place full of love. Any conflict between students was quickly resolved and parents had no problem calling each other to discuss a bully. If so, it was remedied immediately. Our parents grew up together and attended Roy Webb, even our grandparents, so the relationships and bonds were handed down to our generation.

Our classes always had wonderful Christmas parties in December on the last day of school before the break. Sherilyn's mother Connie made wonderful chocolate cookies, Mom would come and help the teacher host the party. All the kids drew names and we tried hard to keep it a secret whose name we had, but I could never make it long without telling. I was eager to please and would tell my victim daily that I got their name and couldn't wait to give them their gift. Of course we probably gave each other $2 gifts, but it didn't matter, the love was there. The respect existed and we truly practiced The Golden Rule at Roy Webb.

Christmas at home with Granny Cochran and our family was amazing. We spent Christmas Eve with the Goodwin's in Ohatchee and then Christmas Day with Granny and the Cochran family. The Cochran family Christmas was huge and I still have the wonderful memories etched forever in my mind. Fifty people or more would pack into my grandmother's single-wide trailer. We didn't mind, there was love and closeness and we just wanted to be together.

Bertie Mae and J.D. Cochran were poor farmers and there was no retirement whatsoever. When J.D. passed away Granny worked for a few years sitting with a wealthy elderly lady in Jacksonville named Mrs. Greenleaf. After my cousin Rhonda was born in 1968, Granny stayed home and helped raise the last group of her grandchildren. She lived on social security and in the late 70s and early 80s that totaled about $150 per month. She was also able to get a few food stamps and collect commodities or government cheese, etc. She didn't have money for gifts for everyone, but she always found a way to make it special. Her kids always gave her money, and she returned it in some way to the grandkids.

Each year, Granny wrapped an individual pair of white socks for each of us. Emily, Myrtle, or my mother would take her shopping and she bought large packs, pulled them out separately and wrapped each pair with a name for every member of her family. At our Christmas gatherings, Granny tossed a wrapped pair of socks to each person and she let us know exactly what her wish was for us. There was not a single person who didn't love those socks. There was something about the socks coming from our Granny. When we would return across the yard to our trailer after the family gathering the first things I did was put my socks on. There just are no words to describe the way those socks made me feel.

CHAPTER FIVE

Nicknames seem to be a southern tradition. I recently polled 50 people randomly and 46 claim ownership of a nickname. Nicknames are generally terms of endearment from loved ones and so we wear them proudly. My Aunt Sylvia is Daddy Bob's older sister and we affectionately call her Wormy. Wormy is a tiny woman and always has been. She met and fell in love with her husband to be in the 1950s at Roy Webb School. Uncle Mac nicknamed his girlfriend and eventual wife Wormy because she was such a tiny little thing. Wormy may be small in stature, but she is larger than life in my world. When Daddy Bob left Mom and I, Wormy stood by Ona Lee. She has never waivered in her loyalty of love for us. She claimed Floyd Ray as her brother-in-law and treats my younger sister, Becky as a niece.

My Aunt Sylvia, aka Aunt Wormy is an angel and as
a young boy I was so blessed to have her.

For many years, Wormy was my only connection to the Gowens family. Wormy was estranged from her father, Thurman Gowens as well, so she understood why my mother was resistant to allow me to visit my biological grandparents. Thurman was rumored to have numerous affairs, crooked dealings, and even commit terrible crimes against female family members. Ona Lee despised him and I grew up hearing the awful stories. Certainly too much information for a young boy, I took it all in, and worried even more.

Wormy was the rainbow in that storm. She was angry with Daddy Bob for leaving us and disappearing from my life. She never made excuses for him. I know that she tried to reach out and encourage him to be part of my life. She advised her younger brother on many occasions what he was missing out on. He rarely listened.

Wormy and her husband Uncle Mac had two children, Donna and Greg, both a good bit older than I. Donna was small like Wormy and beautiful. She has always been tan, fashionable and loving. Greg is tall and handsome. I looked up to him a lot growing up and was thankful that I had the connection with them. Wormy and her family never missed a holiday or birthday without visiting me. She brought gifts for both Becky and I, never making a difference in us. Wormy treated Becky just like she was her biological niece.

As a child I never once longed for toys or the typical trinkets other kids possessed. Between the Cochran's, Goodwin's, and Aunt Wormy, I had just about everything, probably too much. Children of divorce and/or single parent homes often are over-compensated in material belongings and it can mask a yearning for emotional connections they miss out on. Regardless of the material things I had at my finger tips, there was always that yearning for my father and what life might have been like if he had stayed in the picture. I would go months at times and never really miss him, then it would hit me all at once and I wouldn't be able to explain the mood swing or "rapid cycle" to the adults. As a grown up, I have a clearer understanding of my disease and can generally feel my cycles approaching. I reflect on those days as Robby as if I am watching a movie. I see the looks on his face and recognize what he was thinking.

At the age of nine my emotions had taken a toll on my body. I continued to have stomach issues including very irregular bowel movements, constant cramping, and nausea. Mother would run me back and forth to the doctor and he (the doctor) always said I was a normal little boy. There was never any talk of emotions or how often I cried or worried about things. "He's such a worry wart," they would all say. I did panic a lot. I made mountains out of molehills. Once when Granny fell down her steps everyone was trying to help her up, dust her off and make sure nothing was broken, I ran from fence to fence screaming that she was dead. Fear would rush over me in a crisis and I felt blood rush to the top of my head and I would just lose control of my emotions. Rhonda, Sherry, Becky and I would play hide and go seek for hours and if we ever had a hard time finding Becky, I would just collapse and start screaming she had been kidnapped, even though a car hadn't come down the road in an hour. I am sure it had to be exhausting for my family, because it sure was to me.

School let out for the Christmas break my 4th grade year and I hugged Mrs. Delia Williams goodbye and headed for the bus. The usual stomachaches were arising, but we had been preparing for the holiday at school with parties so that meant plenty of candies and cookies. My parents thought I had just eaten too much. I enjoyed a week at home before Christmas Eve and didn't want to tell anyone that I had not been to the restroom in days. Christmas approached and I played as much as possible, but eventually became completely sedentary. By this time, family was convinced it was a case of the flu. Mother had to return to work at the cotton mill on the 27th, and I still had a week of our school break left. She planned to take me to the doctor on the morning of the 28th.

Shortly after my mother left for her night shift I began screaming in pain. Daddy Floyd rushed to my side, picked me up and carried me to the bathroom as I began throwing up straight black bile. He knew it was bad and called the mill immediately telling them to send my mother back home, we were rushing to the emergency room. I was in and out of consciousness but I remember my mother wrapping me in a blanket and holding me in her lap as Dad drove as fast as possible down the Roy Webb Road to Knightens Crossroads and then up US Highway 278 to the Baptist Hospital in Gadsden. I was placed on a cold bed in the ER and I remember sweating and hurting so badly that I couldn't stand it. They took me for X-rays and I had to stand naked in front of a board while a technician took my picture. I wanted to be in my mother's arms. I was scared to death.

The ER Doctor called in a surgeon and they confirmed what my Dad feared, my appendix had ruptured and spilled into my stomach. My Mom says she nearly lost her mind when they gave her little boy only a 40% chance to live through the surgery. The last thing I remember that evening is being pushed on an elevator and seeing my Aunt Emily rushing up to my parents as the doctors wheeled me away.

They cut me down the center from my bellybutton south. I had thirteen staples with some kind of yellow cord intertwining. A tube remained down my throat for nearly a week draining green infection from my abdomen. My mother didn't want to leave my side, not once. She ate beside my bed. She used the restroom in my hospital room. Emily stayed with me for a while why my mother would go outside and visit with four-year old Becky. It was a difficult time for our family, but lots of aunts, uncles, cousins and friends kept us company. One person that I longed for never showed, Daddy Bob.

I was actually quite excited this Christmas because I got a phone call out of the blue in early December from Daddy Bob. He told me he had been in California, but was coming home for Christmas and he had purchased a bright red fire engine for me. It was to be covered in stickers from all the places he had visited. I told everyone I knew. Mother was skeptical but after a phone conversation with Aunt Wormy, it sounded as if he was telling everyone that he was coming home for a visit.

I convinced Mom to take me to the TG&Y in Jacksonville and buy his favorite cologne, Old Spice. When he moved out, there were a few things he left behind; an old pedestal ashtray, a few silver dollars, and a bottle of Old Spice. Mother kept it in a cabinet in the bathroom for years and I would go pull out the white bottle, remove the small red cap, smell of it and think of him. We bought a bright red gift box of

Old Spice and I wrapped it myself. I wrote Daddy Bob on the outside of the package.

As Christmas Eve approached I watched out the window of our trailer every time I heard the sound of tires on the asphalt. I sat on the doorsteps in my coat ready to meet him. He never came. Later when I ended up in surgery I thought for sure that my Daddy Bob would be standing with my mother beside my bed. He was not. Daddy Floyd was standing there, just as he always had been. This was a major turning point. I became extremely bitter toward Bob and at times I took it out on Floyd Ray. I loved Floyd Ray and appreciated him but for some reason I also felt resentment at times. It made no sense and I couldn't control it. Sometimes we resist the people who love us the most and are only trying to help.

When I finally returned home from the hospital I convinced my mother to let me give the Old Spice to Daddy Floyd. He took the gift and opened it with great pleasure. He did everything he could possibly do to fill the void left by Bob Gowens. I know this now and wish that I had accepted it more at that age. I think about the millions of stepchildren in this world and how lucky we all are to have someone willing to step up. Genetics doesn't make a person a father or mother the way genuine love and acceptance does. I guess any man can be a father but it takes a real one to be a Dad.

The spring of 1981 I continued to recuperate from the surgery. I was out of school for six weeks and then had to wear a special bandage across my lower abdomen once I returned to the classroom. Mrs. Williams gave me a ride home each day to avoid having to ride the bus. She drove an Oldsmobile from the 1960s and called her "Lizzie." It was a treat for me to ride shotgun alongside Mrs. Williams. My cousin Tim was in my class but much larger and stronger than me. He carried my books and helped look out for me along with my girl cousins and friends.

By summer, I was fully recovered and ready to put the traumatic experience from Christmas behind me. Aunt Wormy told me that she kept my Dad updated as much as possible on my condition, but I had to just accept the fact that he had moved on with his life and maybe it was better if I did the same. My tenth birthday would mark five years since I last saw him. The big fat woman he ran off with from Piedmont had long since been dumped as well, a second marriage to a lady named Barbara Odell from Hokes Bluff only lasted a few months and rumor was Bob landed somewhere over in West Georgia.

My older stepbrother Tony turned 16 that year and was driving all over creation. We barely saw him and I often wondered if Daddy Floyd missed him. Tony had a wonderful stepfather as well. His mother Betty remarried before Floyd and Ona Lee did. Betty and Rick Shea lived in a beautiful Colonial in downtown Piedmont and owned a Poodle grooming store in Gadsden. Tony had a great life with them and he was kind of a loner. Becky and I probably got on his nerves at that age more than we brought him joy. I wanted to be with him as much as possible, but a sixteen year old has no desire to hang out with a ten year old for sure.

Every summer our family, Granny, Thomas and Emily, Myrtle and Noble and their kids would all go camping together at a lake in Post Oak or on Weiss Lake in Centre. We corralled our campers in a small circle. Granny would take her folding chair to the water as soon as we arrived while her three daughters organized our living space for the next week. Daddy Floyd, Thomas and Noble would set out to catch fish as well and by sun down we would have a good fry going. The next morning we all would awake to the smell of bacon frying at our campsite. Aunt Myrtle was always in charge of breakfast and she would fry pounds of bacon and a couple dozen eggs. She rigged up an oven in her camper, so homemade biscuits were on the menu also.

Rhonda, Sherry, Amy, Becky and I played games for hours, floated in the lake, and squabbled like cousins do. Lee, Myrtle's eldest child was too much older than us to fool with silly kids. He enjoyed fishing and spent a lot of time down by the lake with Granny. Lee was always more mature than anyone else and very reserved. He was tall and skinny and played basketball at Roy Webb and then Jacksonville High School. Myrtle was pregnant with Lee when J.D. died and so he was named Hoyt Lee Lane after Hoyt J.D. Cochran and our mother's eldest brother Hoyt. Lee went on to work in the cotton mill as well for many years while putting himself through nursing school. He was the first in the Cochran family to earn a college diploma and a medical degree.

Our lives revolved around the Cochran family and although Ona Lee, Emily, and Myrtle spent most of their time together, we had nine other first cousins by Bertie Mae's two sons, Hoyt and Charles. We saw them mostly on holidays, Mother's Days and random cookouts throughout the year. The sisters had more in common back then. As women they felt it was their responsibility to take care of Granny and they all doted on her constantly.

The older I got and the more years that passed since Bob left, it became easier for me to pretend that he never existed. I was about to enter a very happy and upbeat time in my life, but the wanderer would stumble back in and bring my progress to a hault.

CHAPTER SIX

The Trouble With Miss Switch, by Barbara Brooks Wallace is one of my favorite childhood books. The book was published in 1972 and later adapted into an animated show. In combination with *Old Yeller* and *Where The Red Fern Grows* I was convinced that I wanted to become a world-renowned author. My fifth grade teacher Mrs. Verna Noah read to the class every day for nearly an hour after lunch. We would turn some of the lights off, settle in our seats and listen to the animated voice of Mrs. Noah. I absolutely loved her and she had dark flowing hair like *Miss Switch*. She was precious and stern at the same time. She was strict yet affectionate. I made straight A's on my report card for the first and only time in my primary education that year.

I can't say enough about how wonderful it was to grow up in and attend a community school like Roy Webb. The best way that I can describe it is like a modern day Little House On The Prairie. I don't ever remember being bullied at that school. I don't remember ever staying angry with another student for more than an hour. Our Principal was a hefty man with a full mustache named Gary Holloway. He and I were buddies from the beginning. I credit my little sister with this. Becky was full of personality and Mr. Holloway and his wife Sandra did not have children. He often told my mother if he ever had a little girl, he would want her just like Becky.

One day Mr. Holloway was teaching our class and my little sister was in Kindergarten. She found an extra apple in her snack sack and thought our Mom had forgotten to pack one for me, so she convinced her teacher to let her venture over to the other side of the school building where my classroom was. Mr. Holloway was sitting on a stool as he often did talking with our class. He always wore long sleeved shirts and a tie. He suffered from Psoriasis and kept his arms covered.

Becky marched in the room, "Bubba...come here!" I was startled and just knew she was about to be in big trouble for interrupting the Principal! Mr. Holloway winked at me, chuckled at her and said, "Becky, can we help you?" She proceeded to tell him with one hand on her hip and the apple in the other that she was there to make sure I had a snack. She explained that she found the extra apple and that our mother worked 3rd shift and had no sleep and was probably confused. Mr. Holloway was so entertained by Becky. I spoke up and told my Sissy that I had my apple. Mr. Holloway advised that she could just give it to him. She replied, "you are way too fat." He roared with laughter as did the entire class. I gasped with embarrassment and sank in my seat. I knew she was done for at that point, but of course Mr. Holloway just patted her on the head and sent her on her way. I told Mom as soon as we got off the school bus that day.

Roy Webb School had been shrank to just an elementary school a couple of years earlier with the addition of the new high school, Pleasant Valley. Several communities came together to form the rural high school outside the city limits of Jacksonville. The city kids went to Jacksonville High School, which was much larger and actually part of the campus of Jacksonville State University at the time. The small communities of Webster's Chapel and Williams closed their schools, Roy Webb and Cedar Springs reduced to elementary classes only and so the new high school was formed. I would have to leave Roy Webb after the sixth grade and take the bus to the new school. I was not looking forward to leaving Roy Webb because it was all I had ever known and I loved it so much. I would rather be in that school building every day than at home back in those days. It was my safe place.

Our sixth grade year we were the seniors and we ruled the school. My cousins Sherry, Amy, Tim and Brenda would all be graduating with me along with my best friends Sherilyn, Stacye, Deborah, Jason, Wendy, Carrie, Carmel, Dale, Seth, Kristie and Chris. These kids were my rock. Many times I wanted to tell them some of the painful thoughts going through my head but I was too embarrassed. I pretended like things were great. I have always been a great pretender. To some degree, I guess that is very dishonest. Even at the age of eleven and twelve I thought about ending my life. I would daydream about what it would have been like if I died during the appendix surgery. I have lived my entire life with destructive thoughts, but was too ashamed to ask for help.

My creativity began to soar in the sixth grade. Mr. Holloway was our spelling teacher and each week he asked us to write a story utilizing each one of our vocabulary words. I asked him if I could bring props for my presentation and he smiled and said sure. I could tell he was excited to see what I had to offer. I brought a bottle of shampoo from my mother's collection. When it was my turn to present my short story, I confidently walked to the front of the room and sat behind the teacher's desk. I delivered a newscast utilizing my spelling words. I took a commercial break and did an advertisement for Finesse Shampoo, thus the need for a prop. The class gave enthusiastic applause at the end of my broadcast. Mr. Holloway was overjoyed with my level of creativity and told me that I needed to hang on to that and one day I could really do something special with my storytelling talent.

After my newscast a group of friends wanted to join in, so we decided to write a soap opera the next week with our spelling words. We performed the show on the stage in the gymnasium for our entire class. I wrote the entire script and we modeled *Search For Hope* after daytime television and primetime shows like *Dynasty* and *Dallas*.

The second half of our school day, Mrs. Lynn Berry our Librarian would become our teacher. She was the most beautiful woman I had ever seen in person. Secretly, I was madly in love with actress Jaclyn Smith, but Mrs. Berry was a close second. She was married to a local veterinarian and I was obsessed with everything about her. She wore beautiful clothes, constantly played with her long flowing brown hair. She could have been the twin of Priscilla Pressley. I was Mrs. Berry's favorite and she made no bones about it. She allowed me to be her teacher's aide in the library and it magnified my love for books and the Dewey Decimal System.

When I say that my group had the run of the school, we surely did. Wendy Geier was the teacher's aide to Mr. Holloway, our principal, so combined with my position in the Library our class did what we wanted to do. We played all up and down the halls and basically had a blast our last year at Roy Webb. One afternoon several of us were playing in the Library and we decided that we wanted to play with a typewriter locked in one of the backrooms. We could see it through a glass window. The window had a rounded cut-out at the bottom like it was an old ticket window. We got the idea that my friends could slide me through that window, then I could unlock the door, and we could play all afternoon with the typewriter. There was not an adult in sight. Mrs. Berry was gone for the day and Mr. Holloway was in his office. The remainder of our class was outside playing. The others lifted my body and feet first. I began to slide into the small hole. I made it all the way to my chin and got stuck. My legs and back were dangling on the other side not touching the ground. It was painful, I began to yell, "I'm stuck, I'm stuck, it hurts!" They tried pulling me back out to no avail. There was nothing to grab hold of except the hair on my head. Wendy Geier ran screaming up the halls to Mr. Holloway's office. Carrie Dempsey, ever the problem solver, was desperately trying to find a way to save me. She pressed my nose flat forcing my chin downward and I slid right through. I remind her every time I see her how she saved my life, ha!

The hefty Mr. Holloway came waddling into the Library with Wendy pulling him as much as she could. He had a look of disappointment on his face, but he was relieved that I was okay. I thought for sure I would be busted, but he just kind of looked me over and made sure that I was okay. He called me at home later that night to make sure that I was not in any pain. He told me to stop letting silly little girls talk me into things. I bit my lip instead of saying, "it was my idea."

As graduation approached I became very emotional. Most of the kids were incredibly excited because we had taken a tour of the new school, gotten our schedules and met some of the new teachers. I felt like a small fish in the ocean at Pleasant Valley(the new school). For years I had been one of the most popular kids at Roy Webb. My mother helped out in the classroom, worked the fall festival, Christmas and Valentines parties, etc. I knew things would be totally different at the high school. Mr.

Holloway told me stories of P.E. class and that I would have to change clothes in the locker room every day. I was not an athletic child by any means. The extent of my sports activities was one year of little league and then playing ball in the yard with my cousins. I was not looking forward to anything about Pleasant Valley.

May of 1984 finally arrived and I realized what I was losing. I sincerely felt a part of my innocence would be gone. All the kids were talking about how we would be split up into different classes. These kids had no idea how in my fantasy world, they were all my brothers and sisters. Spending time with them every day allowed me to escape the terrible thoughts in my head. I was always the weaker kid and I couldn't bare the thought of losing my allies. Life happens and we grow up so I had no choice but to press forward because time was not standing still for me to be ready. I probably would have never been ready.

The final day of school I had a total meltdown and my mother literally had to drag me from the building. I knew my sister still attended Roy Webb and I could come home and visit anytime I wanted, but it wasn't the same. There were a few tears shed by other students, but nothing like me. I literally left kicking and screaming.

The summer in between sixth and seventh grade had its share of challenges. I turned twelve years old as did my girl cousins. Changes were taking place with some of our bodies and we were learning about things we never had before. It was a major transition time in our lives. A kid either thrives during that phase of their life or they suffer greatly.

One summer day, Becky and I were sitting on Granny's plywood porch helping her shuck corn and Mom came walking across the yard from our trailer. She would come home from work at 6:30 AM and go straight to bed and sleep until 1 or 2. She walked up the steps to the porch and looked straight at me. "What did I do," I wondered? She told me that Bob had called and he was over on Hwy 278 at his mother's house and wanted to come for a visit. She told him that it was fine. I couldn't believe it. I had not seen him in seven years and now all of a sudden he was coming to visit. Two and a half years earlier I had nearly died from a ruptured appendix and he never came, but now he is ready to visit. I was shocked that Mom didn't even give me a choice.

Granny encouraged me that it would be okay but I was as nervous as a long tail cat in a room full of rocking chairs. I couldn't be still. Becky really didn't even know who he was but she was planning to tell him off for the way he treated her Bubba. Granny scolded her and informed her she would do no such thing. Daddy Floyd was at work already on the second shift at the mill.

I didn't have to wait very long, within an hour Bob pulled up in a brown and yellow two- toned Dodge truck. He was not alone. Two very tall and slender young men were with him and they both had long hair. They looked like guys from one of the rock bands I had seen on TV. I was quiet and didn't know what to say. Bob introduced the two young men as his stepsons. I don't even remember their name. He was settled in West Georgia now and married to his third wife. She had three grown kids and two of them were standing right there with my father. I was heart broken.

People move on with their lives after a divorce. Life doesn't end for most people who terminate a marriage. Human beings are not wired to live alone or go through life without a mate. I understand as an adult that my father needed a companion and he found one in several different places. I realize that he was a wanderer and had a difficult time settling with anyone. I really didn't blame him as much for divorcing my mother because by now I had seen so much about divorce on television and I knew that my mother had her faults as well. I blamed him for walking away from me. I blamed him for not paying child support and not acting like he was my father. I blamed him for allowing Floyd Ray to take his place in my life. Bob leaving me may have been the best thing for me, but I didn't see it that way. I never really have.

I talked to him a little about school. He missed my graduation from Roy Webb. He made all kinds of promises about what he was going to do nowadays. He would do this better and that better. He gave me a $20 bill. Before they left one of the boys asked my father if Becky belonged to him also and he replied, "no, just the boy." He was married to this family and they didn't even know that I was his one and only child? "Just the boy," is a phrase I will never forget coming out of his mouth. Was he ashamed of me? I never really knew.

The visit was short and honestly I spent several weeks in shock after he left. I felt like something just swooped in and smacked me out of the blue and then ran back into hiding. I didn't understand his ways at all as a young boy, but now I look at myself in the mirror and I see glimpses of him in my own impulsive ways.

CHAPTER SEVEN

Bertie Mae was the youngest of five children and by the mid 1980s she was the only survivor among the siblings. I was only able to meet Uncle John Duncan and his wife Mattie. Unfortunately I was still young when they both died, but Granny kept in touch with John and Mattie's kids and grandkids on a regular basis. They were all active members of the Church of Christ. Uncle John, or "Daddy Dunc," as known to family had been an Elder in the Jacksonville Church and left a long legacy. I believe he was Granny's spiritual influence and leader most of her life and she passed many of his lessons on to me. After John and Mattie's death in the early 80s, Granny became very close to Johnna, their only daughter. Johnna and husband Lee Holder lived in Birmingham where she was a retired teacher. The only time we were ever separated from Granny as children was when she would travel to Birmingham to spend time with Johnna and her family. It was a long distance call back then, but Mom knew I would go out of my mind if I didn't talk to Granny every day, so we were allowed to call her once a day for just a few minutes.

Becky, ever the outspoken one told Johnna on one particular visit that she needed to go and get her own Granny and leave hers alone. They all got a big kick out of that. The remainder of the Duncan family lived "across the mountain" in a backwoods area known as Chinch Creek. Occasionally we would make the drive across Cotaquilla Mountain through Rabbittown and end up in the Hollow. That side of the Duncan family was quite poor and farmed their land much like Bertie Mae and J.D. They were also known as a rough bunch at times and so we really only interacted with the eldest members of the family. Granny had a sister-in-law still living named Aunt Babe. She was married to Tom, Granny's eldest brother. Babe was a sight. She wore long dresses all the way down to her feet, hair in a bun, and a deep voice like a man. She was hard of hearing and yelled every time she spoke.

One of Bertie Mae's nieces gave her an old vase that belonged to a deceased relative. The vase was covered in costume jewelry. Apparently, she had taken broaches, earrings, rings, and any other trinket she could find and glued them to this vase. Granny thought it was beautiful and received it gladly. I thought it was incredibly tacky, but if my Granny wanted it then I was proud that she had it.

She sat the vase on her kitchen table proudly, but it only remained there shortly before a phone call came from across the mountain. Pearlene was the niece of Babe on the opposite side of the family, not the Duncans, so no kin to Granny. Apparently years earlier she had been promised that very same vase and wanted it. Granny explained to her how it came to be in her possession, but Pearlene was belligerent. It had been promised to her and there was no disputing that. Bertie Mae wanted no conflict with anyone from Chinch Creek, so she told Pearlene to come get the vase. "I don't want to do anything wrong," said Granny, "so you just come get it if you say it's yours."

My mother was furious! Ona Lee was ready to whip Pearlene all over the Cove Road when she arrived. There was no way she would allow someone to upset her mother. I was right there with her, planning to let the air out of their tires or something. Granny calmed us down and reminded us that it was not that important. She wanted to do what The Lord would expect from her and that was to give the vase away gracefully. I fought back tears as I watched her take that vase and sit it next to that woman Pearlene stayed and visited for a while and talked about old times and people they had in common. She too wore long dresses and sounded like a man when she spoke. I was glad Ona Lee didn't try and whip her out in the middle of our road, because I think she could have taken Mom.

Pearlene decided it was time to go, she had her vase, so making a run for it was the best bet. She asked Bertie Mae if she could use her restroom before leaving and of course my gracious grandmother pointed down the hall of her trailer. Pearlene remained in the restroom for what seemed like an eternity and I thought maybe her big ole behind had fallen in. Finally she emerged back into the living room/kitchen combo. She stood there facing us and Granny got up and hugged her. She turned to pick up her purse and vase and it was a sight to behold. The tail of her dress was tucked into her panty hose. I about died! It was a full moon.

I ran out the door because I couldn't control my laughter, but Granny just kept a straight face and walked her to the car. As soon as Pearlene left I asked Granny why she didn't tell her about her dress tail and she said, "didn't you hear her say she had to stop at the grocery store? I am sure someone there will tell her, thank you Lord for heaping coals of fire." Later that day and throughout the week I would be outside playing and see Granny standing in her kitchen window washing dishes or cooking and she would just randomly laugh out loud. I never fretted over that ugly vase again and neither did she. The Lord settled the score!

Growing up in the country we were well fed. There was no obsession with weight or healthy cooking because we worked it all off playing in the yard, swimming in the creek, or helping out in the garden. Supper usually was fried meat and four or five vegetables. Ona Lee still has a reputation today for being one of the best cooks in our neck of the woods. She enjoys cooking for large groups of people. Chicken and dressing, chicken dumplings, and a medley of summer vegetables all fried together like green tomatoes, squash, okra and potatoes is her specialty. She calls it "farmers delight."

Bertie Mae was a little more of a minimalist than her middle daughter. One of my favorite things Granny cooked for me was pot roast and cornbread. She had a blue speckled boiler she would sit on the top of the stove to cook her roast in. She didn't need several courses or multiple vegetables to make her happy. When she finished cooking her roast, a piping hot pawn of cornbread would come out of the oven. We crumbled the cornbread on our plates and poured juice from the roast all over it. Just a spoonful of meat is all we needed. The juice-covered cornbread was as good to me as anything. I am sure the fact that it came from Granny just made it even better.

Southern food is nourishment for the soul just like the love of a grandparent. As an adult I have read books on depression, been under the care of 4-6 different Psychiatrists, Therapists, Life Coaches, etc. It's common knowledge that we all deal with emotions differently. How one person reacts to a situation can be completely the opposite of someone else, even in the same family/household. Bertie Mae's conservative Christian background could have caused her to be a judgmental person, but she wasn't. She was a gift from God to people of all walks of life. Occasionally in this world you get to meet those special people that have the ability to see all people equally. She was that kind of woman. She humbled herself before every person she ever met.

I encouraged my grandmother to tell me stories of times gone by. One of the adults might ask me to hush if I brought up J.D. or the youngest son, Luther who both died of cancer in the 1960s, but Granny was always eager to share her stories. She often talked to me about the uncle I never met. Luther was very close to his mother and to Ona Lee.

My grandmother told me that Luther is the reason my mother and father married. Ona Lee began dating Bob in 1964 shortly after J.D. became bedridden. They knew he was going to die and that Luther was also very sick, he had just had one of his legs amputated. Luther spent time at the Children's Hospital in Birmingham, but little was known about pediatric ailments at that time and the resources were limited.

Bob Gowens asked Ona Lee Cochran out on a date while standing in one of the aisles at the cotton mill in town. She knew who he was from attending Roy Webb School, but had never spoken to him. Bob was tall and large. He had a gut on him that would put watermelons to shame. His face was round, a defined pug nose, and wavy hair accented his features. To Ona Lee, he was a nice looking man. Dating was not an option in the Cochran household. J.D. ruled with an iron fist and was very domineering over the entire family. The eldest son, Hoyt was married to Illadene and had already bore five children. Myrtle was next in line and married Noble Lane, she was expecting Lee at the time.

Charles, the second son married 14 year old Helen, who was eight months pregnant with Carl. Ona Lee, Emily and Luther remained at home. My mother quit school and decided to go to work to help the family since J.D. was no longer able to farm. I am not sure she had any choice in the matter even though she disliked school.

Ona Lee was not about to ask J.D. or Bertie Mae for permission to go on a date with Bob Gowens given the current condition of their family and pending tragedy. Myrtle also worked in the mill with Ona Lee, so my Mother simply asked her older sister for permission. Myrtle promised not to tell on her, so Ona Lee had her first date with a boy.

The Gowens family was quite different from the Cochran's. Thurman and Edith Gowens also farmed, but owned their own land and Thurman worked a labor job at the Goodyear plant in Gadsden.

The Gowens family had more money and education than the Cochran's. Bob and Ona Lee became budding lovebirds and the differences in their families, or health crisis couldn't hold them back. J.D. passed away in September of 1964 and Ona Lee was devastated. The strong man who led her through life quickly succumbed to cancer after never really being sick a day in his life. Bob was there to comfort her and serve as a new rock of strength, so of course she fell for him.

Within three months, Luther was on death's door as well. After J.D. died, Bob began visiting Ona Lee at home. He would play checkers for hours with Luther. Ona Lee watched him helping to care for her little brother and she fell more in love. Bob loved Ona Lee and thought she was perfect for him. She was quiet and timid, skinny as a rail, and worked hard. Luther took Bertie Mae by the hand and asked her to allow Bob and Ona Lee to marry. He thought Bob would be a wonderful husband to his sister. Bertie Mae gave her daughter permission. Standing in the Gowens living room, Bob and Ona Lee became one. Bertie Mae was not able to come to the wedding due to Luther's condition, so Uncle John and Aunt Mattie Duncan filled in for her.

Bertie Mae sat in her porch swing and told me the story of how my mother and father met every time I asked. She articulated the details so well that I could almost imagine myself there. Granny always told me that I would make a great storyteller when I grew up. I learned everything from her. All I had to do was ask a question about the old days and she would rock back and forth with her legs crossed, lay her head over to one side against the chains, and delight me detail by detail.

There were rumblings in the family about Granny making a difference between me and the other grandkids. Every now and then, I would hear someone said this or that, "Granny talks about Robby more than any other kid", or "Granny spends all her time with Robby and Becky." Bertie Mae always told me, "you make the difference, Sugar, not me. You make the difference." I think she meant that she treated me differently because I needed her so much more than the rest. It wasn't like she never had anything to do with others, or made a difference with her thoughts or love for one more than the other. She spent more time with me because I needed her and she lived right there in the same yard with us. I craved her attention and I got it.

The summer of 1984 drew to a close. I confided in Granny just how nervous and worried I was to start the new chapter of life at Pleasant Valley. She told me it was all part of growing up and if I just remembered the things I learned in Sunday School and applied them to my life, I would be fine. I knew about the power of prayer and just like Granny taught me, I never went to sleep without talking with The Lord.

CHAPTER EIGHT

I have heard many people say in life they would do things differently if they had the chance to go back in time. Others stand firm that every experience made them the person they are today and they have no regrets. I have plenty of regrets, but I would never go back to Junior High again. Even with what I know now, I don't have the emotional resolve to face those years again. It's painful just writing about it. I was not prepared at all for adolescence. Is anyone ever really prepared?

My classmates from Roy Webb and I were scattered at Pleasant Valley. We passed each other in the hallways and many of them were able to make new friends right away. A few kids from my Church and Sunday School class were also at Pleasant Valley, so I did have friendly faces scattered through my days. The issue was not the school or the kids, it was me. I was awkward, nerdy, and had very low self-esteem.

In my adult life I have written and spoken a great deal about anti-bullying initiatives. Kids can be cruel, but they also don't really know how to handle other kids with different personalities, mood swings, or uncontrollable awkwardness. The root of bullying in schools truly begins at home. We all need to teach our children to be as accepting of others as possible regardless of any differences. From my perspective at that age, I also needed to be more confident and make an effort to get to know the kids who bullied me. I approached junior high with a negative attitude. I went in already feeling defeated.

Each of my cousins excelled in their new relationships and I felt left out for the first few years.

I was not comfortable with learning about sex, the changes my body was going through, and I wanted to hold my loved ones back as well. It was a constant emotional struggle. Bipolar Disorder is easier to understand and somewhat control as an adult, but as an adolescent I seemed to be spiraling out of control constantly. My parents noticed my declining grades, but there was never any question about mental health or the root of my problems.

I don't remember a day of junior high where someone didn't push or shove me in the hall, accuse me of being homosexual, or call me vile names. I just didn't understand how all of a sudden my safe place had transitioned into this jungle. I missed Roy Webb and Pleasant Valley made me hate school. It wasn't the building again, it was me. It was my own outlook on life, my personal struggles, and lack of treatment. I bottled everything inside and became too ashamed to tell anyone how much I was suffering. I made the mistake once of telling my mother about being picked on and she marched right up to the school and talked to the Principal. By the time the guilty party was notified, I was the talk of the school as a snitch. It just made things worse, so I tried to hide everything else. I was spat on constantly, pushed down stairs, punched, popped with rubber bands, and verbally ridiculed. Planning my own suicide was the only thing I could think to do.

I lost count of the number of times I wanted to commit suicide between the ages of thirteen and sixteen. Fortunately, I was too cowardly to carry anything out, but it was dangerous for me to sit and think about it. I knew from Bible study that taking your own life would send you straight to Hell, so I used that doctrine to talk myself out of those thoughts. Bertie Mae could tell a major change in my behavior. I was moody and withdrawn. Many times I would sit beside her in the swing with tears streaming down my face. I never could tell her everything that was on my mind, only bits and pieces. I also lashed out at my stepfather repeatedly during this time. Ona Lee and Floyd Ray went through their own trials in marriage during this time and there was a lot of uncertainty in our home. He even moved out for several months. Sometimes I would get angry at him and say, "you're not my daddy," and he would reply with equal disdain, "if I am not, you don't have one."

Depression and mental struggles can make a person very narcissistic. We become so wrapped up in our own problems that we can't wrap our head around the truth that everyone has struggles. Chemical imbalances prevent people from bouncing back from sadness as quickly as others, so I know that there are many times I can't help how I feel, but I do recognize that it makes me somewhat selfish. I never hold my loved ones accountable for my feelings, because I know they don't understand my disease if they have not experienced depression or mental illness on their own.

Looking back, I wish that I had another male around my age to really look up to. Tony was six years older and had gone about living his life. We rarely heard from him and even went a few years without seeing him. He and Floyd Ray had some sort of argument and he distanced himself. Most of the cousins my age were girls. They were my only influence. I had one male cousin in my classroom all those years at Roy Webb, Tim Cochran. He was the youngest son of my uncle Charles and aunt Helen. Tim and I were as different as daylight and dark. He was fearless, tough, rough, and rambunctious. He was very popular with the other kids at Pleasant Valley, and a great deal more mature than I, so we had nothing in common. I loved him, but getting older made us grow apart and we were just not interested in the same things. Tim could drive a car before I could ride a bicycle.

After a couple of years at Pleasant Valley, the Calhoun County Board of Education decided to complete their initial plan for our rural area of the state. They would completely close Roy Webb and Cedar Springs Elementary Schools and merge them into Pleasant Valley. My community was devastated as they did not want to lose Roy Webb. My mother wanted Becky to attend Roy Webb through the sixth grade just like I had and many of our family. The board members agreed to hear our concerns at a community meeting at the school building. A couple hundred parents, grandparents, and students showed up for the meeting in the Roy Webb gymnasium.

Sherilyn Johnson and I sat on the bleachers and watched our parents listen to the board members and express their concerns about expanding Pleasant Valley and closing a school that had been such an influence on many families in our area. Sherilyn and I both loved Roy Webb and treasured the time we spent there together. While the meeting was in progress I noticed my older cousin, Sharon standing in a doorway between the gym and office and it appeared that she was crying. She was waiving to get my mother's attention. A teacher sitting behind my mother got up and went to see what was wrong. After a few words were spoken, the teacher quickly walked to my mothers seat and whispered in her ear. My mother jumped up, grabbed my sister by the hand and ran out the door. I looked at Sherilyn and told her something is wrong in my family and I ran down the bleachers and toward the door. As I reached the sidewalk in front of the school I looked to the left and saw my mother collapse on the sidewalk in screams. My older cousins were surrounding her and trying to hold her. My heart sank and I just knew that my Granny was dead.

I ran to my family. My mother was screaming uncontrollably. I began asking "is it Granny, is my Granny dead?" My older cousin, Danny grabbed me by the shoulders and told me no Granny was fine, it wasn't her. It was my cousin Tim. He was in a motorcycle accident and it killed him. I couldn't believe it. Tim was fifteen years old now and had his entire life ahead of him. He was such an amazing boy. I envied his tenacity and confidence. I immediately thought of his parents, Charles and Helen. His sister Diane and brother Carl, they must have been ready to die right beside him. I thought about Granny and we had to get home to her.

The day before Tim's death was actually Charles' birthday. Granny couldn't reach her middle son on his birthday so she called him the next afternoon, shortly after Tim had been killed, but before anyone notified her. We were all at the school so she was home alone. She could tell there was something wrong in Charles' voice. When Granny wished him Happy Birthday a day late, he knew that she did not know about his son's tragic death. He told his mother that he couldn't talk and that something was terribly wrong but someone would be there to tell her shortly. Granny walked out to her front porch, sat on her swing and began to pray. The eldest son, Hoyt and two of his grown sons pulled in her drive way. She met them at the steps and told them she knew there was bad news.

By the time we made it back home to Cove Road the sun was down and the sky was completely dark. I ran to Granny's porch, but Uncle Hoyt just put his hand up and asked me to stop for a second. Granny was sitting in her swing, rocking back and forth, softly crying and praying. It broke my heart to see her there. I know Tim's death at the young age of fifteen brought back all the pain from losing Luther at the same age. I just wanted to be with her and take care of her. She opened her eyes and motioned for me to come to her. I ran to her and wrapped my arms around her. She knew I was more worried about her than anyone else and she whispered in my ear, "Granny's okay, The Lord always takes care of me."

Ona Lee and her other siblings were constantly aggravating my grandmother about sitting in her swing sleeping all day, but I knew she used that swing to talk to The Lord. It was her place to reflect and meditate. We all have our favorite place to quietly talk to our Savior. That white wooden porch swing was Granny's place. She found the peace that passes understanding in that spot. It was natural for her to retreat there in such a tragic time.

The days and weeks that followed Tim's death were difficult for our entire family. This tragedy changed everything. Watching Charles and Helen bury their youngest child still haunts me today. It was so unfair. I didn't understand why God would see fit to take him. In the south when someone dies, we often explain it away by saying everyone has a time to go. This is true, life always ends in fleshly death, but a tragedy that takes the life of a vibrant young boy seems unimaginable. I can't help but wonder today, twenty-five years later how this could be part of an almighty plan.

Ten years earlier I experienced the death of Floyd Wesley Goodwin, my Paw Paw, and several elderly aunts and uncles had passed away from long diseases, heart attacks, etc., but Tim's accidental death was the first time my cousins and I had really experienced this kind of loss. For those around my age, it was really a loss of innocence for each of us. We began to really have to consider our own mortality. For me, it compounded my fears of losing Bertie Mae and other relatives. If it could happen to Tim, it could happen to anyone in the family.

Within a few months of Tim's death, my Aunt Wormy gave Mom a call with sad news of her own. Thurman Gowens passed away from a long illness. Even though Wormy didn't have a relationship with her abusive father, she was there during his illness to support Edith, her mother. Wormy offered to take me to the funeral home if my mother would allow it, but I didn't want to go. I was still too raw from Tim's death and I had never met my biological grandfather. I only heard bad stories about him and had no desire to see him lying in a casket. I felt bad for Bob that his father was gone, but I was also still angry with him. I had not seen him in three years, since he brought his two new stepsons for the visit.

By the age of fifteen I began to grow out of my awkwardness and settle into friendships at Pleasant Valley. I started thinking about college and what I wanted to do with my life. Grades improved, self-confidence increased, and I felt that I had a game plan. Many of my friends were experimenting with sex, drugs, alcohol, and smoking, but I was still pretty straight laced and had avoided the peer pressure. Mother kept us sheltered at home and I didn't go out with friends or have sleepovers. She really didn't trust her kids staying at someone else's house unless they were family.

My mood swings seem to regulate after turning sixteen. I had more to look forward to, including driving, planning for college and beginning my life as a man. Most of my sadness over the lack of a relationship with my father was replaced by anger and resentment. My childhood was almost gone and I was totally over it. I daydreamed occasionally about being his friend as an adult, maybe going fishing, or to a baseball game, but I gave up on the dream of Bob being a "daddy" to me.

CHAPTER NINE

By 1989 I was in my senior year at Pleasant Valley High School. My self-confidence still waivered, but for the most part, I didn't hate school anymore. Once my classmates and I got through the awkwardness of puberty, life seemed to improve. The boys who stuffed me in trashcans, pushed me down the stairs, and refused to pick me for their teams in P.E. class were now my friends. At home, Floyd Ray and Ona Lee seemed to work out most of their differences and our family unit was once again functioning well. The older I got the more my mother seemed to respect me and allow me to make my own decisions. I think she realized what a great kid I was since I never got in any trouble at school. She allowed me to date a very sweet girl named Mary. Mary and I attended the prom together, loved to go to McDonalds and a movie. I had a side job cutting grass for a couple of elderly people in the mill village in Jacksonville.

Orville Johnson was our school counselor and all during the senior year we took the A.C.T. test, applied for scholarships, and determined what we wanted to pursue in life. I knew that I wanted to be a writer, but also realized the practical approach would be to have a degree I could fall back on. I decided that I would pursue Broadcast Journalism. I was fortunate to be the only high school senior in Calhoun County to land an internship at TV40 in Anniston. I worked with local anchors after school preparing newscasts, filming local commercials, and even got to sit behind the anchor desk for a couple of newsbreaks.

I continued to write short stories, book ideas, and scripts in high school. Sherilyn Johnson, my best friend from elementary school was my biggest fan and supporter. For four years in high school I wrote a soap opera called "Opposite Worlds." I penned a new script each week and Sherilyn couldn't wait to get her hands on it. I was too embarrassed to put it out there with too many students, but God knew I needed a Sherilyn in my life, she pushed and encouraged me with positive comments about my creativity and writing style from day one.

Close friends including Sherilyn Johnson truly helped me to overcome the awkwardness and fear at Pleasant Valley High.

In high school I had a love for math. My two favorite teachers were Ms. Sharon Padgett and Mrs. Regina McCurry. They both inspired a great love for math and competing in the county tournament. My senior year I finished first on our Calculus team from Pleasant Valley and won the Math Student of the Year award. I was determined to have a bright and successful future. Every conversation I had with Aunt Wormy, I would ask her, "Do you think Daddy Bob would be proud?" Wormy always encouraged me and told me that yes he was proud, but it didn't matter if he was or wasn't, she thought I hung the moon and stars and she always treated me that way.

Mother and Daddy Floyd were extremely proud as well and as I approached graduation they encouraged me to pursue my dreams at our local university, Jacksonville State. I would have loved to enroll at the University of Alabama. Dad and I loved Alabama football and we watched the games religiously every fall. I was such a fanatic about Alabama football growing up I would actually cry when they lost a game. (I still do that today).

The cotton mills were steady employment but it wasn't enough to pay for tuition at JSU so I knew that my parents would not be able to afford to send me to college. I planned to live at home and get a job to cover my expenses at school. I would graduate with honors and a Cum Laude diploma but it wasn't enough to gain a scholarship. The greatest example my parents, grandmothers, and relatives set for me was hard work. There would never be any question about work ethic in our family. Hard work was engrained in our character from a very young age. Even though my goal was to pursue a white-collar career, the same time and effort would be applied if it had been a hard labor position.

As the spring of 1990 approached my mother asked me if I planned to invite Daddy Bob to my graduation. Of course I wanted to. I wanted to show him what I had accomplished. I would be wearing a gold stole, gold and black honor cords, and a special pen for Math honors at my graduation. I wanted to show Bob just how successful I was in school and what he had missed by not being a part of my life. We prepared the invitations and mailed it to his home in Whitesburg, Georgia. Since Thurman Gowens was dead, Mom encouraged me to invite Edith Gowens, my paternal grandmother. I had never met her and was eager to get to know her. Mother had nothing nice to say about Thurman or Edith, but she was willing to be cordial for me.

Aunt Wormy was ecstatic that I invited her mother to the graduation and agreed to make sure she was able to attend. Of course all the Cochran's were in attendance because my cousins Amy, Sherry and Brenda were graduating as well. It was sad for our family that Tim would not be there. Two years had passed since his accident and I felt deep remorse and pain for Charles and Helen because I knew how much they missed their youngest child.

Daddy Floyd's family, The Goodwin's were all in attendance supporting me as they had since I was three years old. Aunt Irma and Uncle Doug cheered me on as "ponce-a-time" during the graduation ceremony. As my classmates and I walked into the gymnasium to the tune of "Pomp and Circumstance," I saw Bob Gowens with the rest of my family. He looked old and tired. He wore a suit and matching hat. The suit was an old western material and made of polyester. I knew it was probably the best he could do. His dreams of becoming a wealthy world traveler had not come to fruition. Material possessions are not the most important things in life, but to a teenager who heard stories all of his life about the dreams of his wandering father, I felt regret for him. I felt sorry for him that his dreams had not come true. I didn't want to end up that way.

Daddy Bob's wife and stepchildren did not attend the graduation with him and I was glad. I was not open to a relationship with them at that time because I was still immature and bitter. My family cheered me on and I enjoyed the loud applause and support as I walked across the stage and received my diploma from our Principal, Mr. Wayne Wigley.

The family gathered in our small trailer on the Cover Road after the ceremony. The Goodwin's and Gowens' were blended for the first time all in support of their little Robby. It was a great feeling and everyone seemed to get along really well. Daddy Bob was proud and he told me several times just how much he loved me and respected what I had accomplished. I earned over $600 in cash gifts from my family members. The first semester at JSU would cost me $550, so I felt that I was in good shape. My card from Daddy Bob was empty except a short note from Barbara, his wife. She congratulated me and told me they wanted me to become a member of their family and get to know them.

Bob told me that he was working on a graduation gift for me and that he would be getting with me about it in the next couple of weeks. I am not sure what I expected from him, but I was a little surprised and disappointed that he couldn't' even spot me a $20 toward my tuition. I didn't say anything to him about it, but I complained to my mother later. Of course she reminded me that he had never supported me financially and that we had made it just fine. Granny Gowens (Edith) and I hit it off immediately. She was not like my Granny Cochran or Maw Maw Goodwin as far as affection. She was a little more sophisticated and didn't show as much love, but I did enjoy meeting her and having great conversation. I could tell that she was impressed with my accomplishments and she asked me to come visit and I agreed that I would soon.

I noticed that my father and his mother, Eidith did not have a lot of interaction. It confirmed for me that he was just as Wormy had always explained, estranged from his immediate family just as he was from me.

Within one month after my graduation I was working two jobs. Ms. Padgett, my math teacher was a first-cousin of Bill Bussey, a radio station owner in our community. Bill hired me to be a weekend DJ on AM810, Jacksonville's Classic Country. During the week I worked as a cashier at Taco Bell. I began saving money for my books and a new wardrobe for college.

In July of 1990 I was getting dressed for a shift at Taco Bell and the phone rang. Back then there was no caller I.D. so conversations were more spontaneous and unrehearsed. I was pleasantly surprised to hear Daddy Bob's voice on the line. Even though he promised at graduation that he would be "getting with me" regarding a gift, I didn't expect to hear back from him. We talked briefly about my two jobs. He seemed unimpressed and a little rushed for time. I was rushed as well because I needed to get to work. Bob informed me that he had purchased a very expensive remote controlled airplane as my gift and thought I could go into the pasture across from our trailer and fly it as a hobby.

I didn't mean to disrespect my father, but I laughed at his offer for my gift. I lost control of my temper. All the years of frustration and stress emptied on him at that moment. I explained to him that I was working two jobs to save the money I needed for school, to avoid student loans. I advised him that I had very little free time and even if I did I had no desire to fly a remote controlled airplane. He was equally tempered and told me the toy was worth $750. Really? I thought wow I could really use $750 right now. That would pay for an entire semester and books at JSU. The last words my father ever said to me were "I am not about to give $750 to some eighteen year old." I laid the phone back on its base gently, walked to my car and drove to work.

In my mind, I was not an average eighteen year-old. I was responsible and never been in any trouble. At that age, I had never had a drink of alcohol, no cigarettes, and no drugs. I made good grades, graduated with honors, got two jobs after high school, and was enrolled at JSU's School of Communication. Bob Gowens had never known me and he never would. I was angry, hurt, disgusted and done. He never called back.

A couple of days later I sat in the swing with Bertie Mae and we talked about my Dad. Bertie Mae never spoke a word of negativity about him as I was growing up. She didn't like the fact that my mother told me of his extramarital affairs, wandering spirit, and drinking problem. She didn't want me to be influenced about Bob in any way. At my graduation, she and Bob embraced several times and I overheard him tell her how much he loved and respected her and was sorry that he had let her down. Granny was the most forgiving woman ever, but she was genuinely disappointed and angry with Bob for his last conversation with me. She cried with me and begged me once and for all to just let him go and move on with my life. Hearing Bertie Mae say it was time to move on from the hope and dream of one day really having a relationship with Bob was what I needed to close that chapter.

My college career began in September and I embraced my new journey. I attended school from 7:30 AM to 1:30 PM each day, came home and changed into my Taco Bell uniform, and worked until 2:00 AM most mornings. From the age of eighteen onward, I never worked less than forty hours a week. I was determined to accomplish my education and career goals.

I began to visit Granny Gowens at least once every few months for a while. I told her about my conversation with Bob. She was not angry at him, she blamed it on his current wife, Barbara. "She is the reason he never came to see you," Granny would say. She claimed that Barbara controlled everything he did. None of that information changed the way I felt. He didn't even marry Barbara until I was twelve years old and I didn't respect a man who would allow some woman to control whether he saw his biological son or not.

"Once aponce a time", this large and jolly man gave me a record. On one side of the record was a chipper song with the title, "How Much Is That Doggy In The Window," but on the other side a somber version of "Daddy Don't Go," played. Bob gave me the record at age four or five, before the name change, before the event that would onset my life long battle with depression and Bipolar Disorder. I am not sure who had the idea to market two totally different songs on one 45 record. Looking back now it does seem ironic because I have two varying personalities, one very happy and high strung, and one very sad and somber. I don't have any idea where that record is now, but it is the story of my young life, thanks to Bob.

CHAPTER TEN

The town of Jacksonville, AL is just the kind of place you would want to raise your children. Nestled in the foothills of the Piedmont and Lookout Mountain ranges, Jacksonville is about 60 miles northeast of Birmingham and 120 miles west of Atlanta. From the beautiful town square you can see the thirteen-story Houston Cole Library and other architecturally beautiful structures on the campus of Jacksonville State University. The Gamecock Inn, named for the mascot of JSU sits on the south end of town along with Wal-Mart and most of the retail shops. The campus stretches east to west at the north end of the city limits. The Roy Webb community is about ten miles northwest of the campus. I had a very short commute each day to class in the 1984 Oldsmobile Cutlass Supreme I bought with my income from Taco Bell and AM810 radio.

By the time I was a junior at JSU I had switched my major to management and marketing, let the radio gig go and moved up to a salaried assistant manager position with Taco Bell, under the parent company, Pepsico. I took advantage of the Pepsi reimbursement program for college tuition for their full time employees and life was good. Even though I had given up on broadcasting at the time, I continued to write and create book ideas, but my success in business motivated me to switch to what I thought at the time was a much more practical degree.

As young people I think we are always anxious to leave home and start new beginnings. Growing up I often heard lyrics in country songs about "one horse towns." I felt that way about Jacksonville at the time and I had my sights on the big city lights. I didn't want to leave my mother or Granny, but I had shucked all the corn and shelled all the peas I wanted to. I began telling everyone grandeur ideas of fortune and fame as I conquered the world. When my mood would swing to a high level of energy, there was nothing I wouldn't try to accomplish and certainly nothing I would not boast about. I grew into a mighty young man who for a while, forgot of the lost little boy from Roy Webb.

I sewed my oats in a good way as a young college student. A great friend from high school named Ken Bryant and I became best friends in college. We were both just good ole boys from the country and he really helped me to become a better dude. I needed the testosterone in my life that had always been surrounded by overflowing estrogen. Ken and I would tear up the town cruising his Ford Thunderbird up and down Broad Street in Gadsden. We followed the JSU Gamecocks across the southeast and enjoyed a National Championship in our division in 1992, the same year Gene Stallings returned The Crimson Tide of Alabama to glory.

My older brother Tony and I also reunited and he began coming back around the family and we all had a wonderful time together. It was as if he never left. I had wonderful relationships in my early twenties and I am so thankful my older brother and younger sister were among those. I was busy, successful and happy. Bob Gowens was far from my mind.

In 1994 I took a position with a retail jewelry chain as a Store Manager. I had the education and experience of a leader and was grateful that I was recognized for the hard work and accomplishment. When I applied for the job, Bertie Mae sat in her swing with me and prayed that I would get the position and yes I did. She was a little sad that I was being relocated to the town of Huntsville, AL about a two-hour drive north of Jacksonville. Huntsville is home of a booming Aerospace industry including several NASA facilities. I was excited to try something new at the age of 22 and enjoy my first experiences away from home. I missed Granny and my other family members and friends as well, but I was excited about the new beginnings.

Granny never traveled much in her life. Her short trips to Birmingham were the extent of her "vacations" or sight seeing. Growing up in rural

Alabama as a poor farm girl, Bertie Mae did not have those kinds of experiences or desire. I invited her to come home with me to Huntsville for a couple of days and she was ecstatic. She wanted to see where I lived, worked, and even told me, "Sugar, I just want to see where you sit when we talk on the phone so that I can imagine you there." I couldn't wait to entertain Granny in my apartment on Sparkman Drive in Huntsville.

Granny and I loaded up my 1993 Nissan pickup truck and headed north. As we approached the town of Guntersville I told Granny not to be frightened but we were about to cross a large body of water. I drove onto the large bridge overlooking the Tennessee River and Granny sat straight up in the passenger seat looking around wide-eyed with amazement. She turned to me and said "this must be what they call the ocean?"

I laughed uncontrollably at Granny for a moment and explained to her it was just the river. She didn't like my making fun of her and reminded me that she had never been anywhere in her life, how was she to know? Immediately the wheels in my mind started to turn. I had seen the ocean. We took a family trip without Granny when I was 16 to Myrtle Beach and I remember the amazing feeling I got the first time I saw the ocean and I wanted my 86 year-old Grandmother to have that experience as well. When we got home from Huntsville, I asked if she would travel to the beach with me and of course she told me she would go with me anywhere!

Two weeks later I took a vacation from my job, booked us a hotel at the beach and picked my sweet Granny up. My mother and her sisters didn't like the idea at all of me hauling Granny off six hours from home just she and I. What if she had a heart attack or stroke? What if she fell and broke her hip? She didn't care, she wanted to be with me and I wanted to be with her. My friends and coworkers couldn't believe that I was taking my elderly grandmother to the beach. I should be partying with girls, drinking friends under the table, and dancing all night at Spinnaker on the coast. No, it wasn't my style, I wanted to be with Granny and I wanted to share this experience with her more than anything.

We arrived at the coast and Granny couldn't see what she was about to experience just yet due to the tall hotels on Front Beach Road. My excitement was building. We pulled into our hotel and walked into the lobby. I booked a room with a balcony on the eighth floor, so our view would be amazing. We carried our small bags to the elevator for the ride up. She was so casual in that moment, so relaxed. She really didn't have a clue just how amazed and taken aback she was about to feel. I knew that she was about to see one of God's most amazing creations and I just couldn't contain myself. I opened the door to our room, ushered her in and threw the bags on one of the double beds. We walked toward the sliding glass doors to the balcony and I took her by the hand. I led her onto the balcony and when she caught her first glimpse her mouth opened wide and she literally stumbled backwards.

Tears streamed down my face as she gripped the railing on the balcony to steady herself. I have never had a more unique experience. It is the single most beautiful moment and memory of my life. I would trade every exciting experience that I have ever known to have that moment and to be able to describe to you just how amazing it was. This woman loved The Lord and I got to be there when she saw one of the most amazing creations for the first time. We were both breathless and speechless.

For two days and nights we sat on the balcony listening to the waves, watching the seagulls and taking short walks on the beach. The sand was a little too much for her and it was hard to keep her balance, but we walked arm and arm. I have a photo that I treasure of the two of us walking arm and arm. She has her cane in her spare hand and I was carrying my sandals in mine. My sweet friend Artist Gina Brown painted a beautiful picture for me of that photo. It is my greatest treasure.

As long as I live, I'll never forget my walk on the
beach with my precious Bertie Mae.

Many people have told me how the ocean is therapeutic for them. It is for me to this day and every time I go, I remember those days, that trip, and the wonderful bonding between Robby and Bertie Mae. We would have stayed there forever if possible.

On our drive home Granny told me that she had always had a hard time imagining what Heaven would look like and feel like. "They say we just can't imagine how beautiful and peaceful Paradise will be," she explained. "For me when I think about Heaven now, it will be that far off place where the sky meets the water. We will walk the shores together one day," she said while holding my hand. I knew at that moment that I couldn't let her down. I needed to make sure regardless of what obstacle I faced in life that I made it to the Pearly Gates so that I could walk the shores of Heaven with my Granny. I had put off for too many years what I knew I needed to do, so soon after that trip, I took a walk down the aisle and obeyed the Gospel, receiving my gift of salvation from The Savior. As I was baptized, I saw the tears streaming down Bertie Mae's face and I knew just how happy and proud she was and exactly what this moment meant to her.

I didn't stay in Huntsville very long. I was incredibly lonely and the retail company I worked for began closing many of its mall stores. Shortly before I moved tragedy struck our hometown and family once again. A series of tornadoes came through and wiped out the north end of our community, destroying a Methodist Church and killing twenty-two men, women and children. I was safe in Huntsville and unaffected by the weather of Palm Sunday, but I was frantic not being able to reach my family for nearly twenty-four hours. It was an awful feeling to be away from them during a crisis. Just a few months later a tragic car accident rocked the Cochran family again. I couldn't understand how my Uncle Charles could handle anymore after losing Tim, but now he had to bury Helen. She and her best friend perished when a transfer truck crossed the median and hit them head on. Aunt Helen was a young and energetic woman of only 45 years old when she was killed. Her two remaining children, Carl and Diane were devastated. Even though they both had married and bore children, losing their mother in such a horrific way is still unimaginable. I found another job and moved back home before the end of that year, one horse town or not, I wasn't ready to be that far from Jacksonville.

Many people with a creative imagination can move to different areas of the world and thrive. Writers even need that at times to find inspiration. My mental health has always prevented me from being successful when I am away from my family. Even though I was a big talker as a child, "I will do this and I will do that. I will live in London, Paris, Rome...," the truth is that I need my family to survive. I still didn't understand my impulsive behavior and mood swings, I just knew that I needed to feel safe and loved and Jacksonville was where I found it.

(1)

Bertie Mae standing on the balcony overlooking the Gulf of Mexico. It was the most amazing experience of my life witnessing my 86 year old grandmother seeing the beach for the first time.

Chapter Eleven

One of the motivating factors for me in the field of management has been the title. It's self-serving and narcissistic at times, but I like companies that promote their employees and honor them with nice titles. One of the greatest titles I ever earned was "Best Man." Ken Bryant decided to marry the lovely young lady he was dating and he asked me to stand beside him on that magical day. Ken's bride had a sweet little daughter from a previous relationship and he was madly in love with mother and child. I was also dating a gorgeous girl from Gadsden named Sonja and she too had a precious daughter, Haliegh.

Being raised by a stepfather I felt right at home as a father figure to little Haliegh. Sonja and I dated for three years and integrated our families quite well. I landed a job in public relations and felt that my career was headed in the right direction so a family seemed like the natural next step.

Not too long after our family suffered the loss of Aunt Helen, a heart attack from out of nowhere claimed the life of Thomas Hill, married to Aunt Emily. Thomas had been a solid male figure in my life from the moment I was born. He was not only Daddy to Rhonda and Sherry, but treated me as his little boy as well. When Daddy Floyd married my mother, Uncle Thomas put his finger in his face and told him, "you will never hurt Robby or you will deal with me." Of course, Thomas and Floyd Ray got along just fine and became as great of friends as Thomas and Bob were. Emily, Rhonda and Sherry were devastated. We all were in shock and never expected to lose Thomas. I was forced to once again realize my own mortality and just how life was moving at a fast pace.

Losing Thomas was definitely like losing a second parent and I felt pressured to settle down and get on with life. I looked to Sonja to fill that emotional void and uncertainty about life.

My mother and Daddy Floyd seemed to jive well with the pending in-laws so I proposed and Sonja accepted. There was not much excitement surrounding the announcement of my nuptials. Family members seemed surprised that I had actually found someone and was ready to marry. I was known for being impulsive and I think most of my aunts and uncles felt that it was exactly what I was doing. Ken married and was settled in nicely with his new family as well and some of my close relatives and friends thought I was just doing it to "fit in."

To this day I still really can't put my finger on just what happened in those three months leading up to the April wedding, but I panicked. Some voice deep inside just kept telling me that at the age of 24 I was not as ready as I thought I was. Maybe I was seduced by the thought of an immediate family. The success of my career meant it was time to have everything that any red blooded American boy would want.

I never cheated on Sonja but I was not faithful when it came to honesty and true feelgns. I was not ready and I knew it on Christmas Day when I put the engagement ring on her finger. It was another one of those impulsive decisions. It was another impulsive decision the night that I walked out of her apartment and never looked back. I broke her heart and I have never gotten over it and I have never had that kind of relationship with a woman again. I do believe that I was in love, but love is not enough especially if you are not mentally stable.

I suffered a lot of emotional pain for months after I broke Sonja's heart. She eventually married and divorced and moved on with her life and today we are friends, but at that time I wondered if I was any better than Bob. I made a visit to my Grandmother, Edith Gowens and we had a long and deep conversation about my impulsive father. Granny Gowens told me that Thurman was a womanizer and so was Bob. She begged me to be careful and not treat women the way those men did. She told me stories of horror in what she had to live in and confirmed most everything my mother had previously said about Thurman and

Bob. Granny Gowens had no insight as to why my Dad was so absent and impulsive. It was a cycle that she did not want to see me repeat and I appreciated her candor. I left with a new respect for her.

I gained the title of Uncle this same year. My little sister Becky gave birth to my nephew Austin Ray Pruitt. I certainly wasn't ready for my 18 year old little sister to become a mother, but Austin brought tremendous joy into our family and created a bond between Ona Lee and Floyd Ray that many of our family had not seen for years. Becoming grandparents certainly mellowed the two of them. I have been able to witness just how a special grandchild can soften the firm and previously unbending ways of an adult. To say Austin wrapped his grandparents around his two little fingers is a huge understatement.

I threw myself into my work and decided to focus on building a career and future that I could be proud of. Enjoying a romantic or personal life became a distant thought. Although I began to enjoy great professional growth and success, 1997 proved to be a desperately challenging year of closure.

September 22, 1997 was a normal Monday for me. I had meetings in Birmingham at our corporate office and didn't make it home until nearly 7 PM. I had supper at my mother's home, watched TV and then walked across the yard to my mobile home, now parked behind my mother. I called Bertie Mae to check on her and say good night. I settled in to watch some television. Simultaneously in Whitesburg, Georgia at his small mobile home, Bob Gowens was arriving home from a hard day at work. His battle with Diabetes seemed to be getting worse, including restricted vision, high blood pressure, and even more weight gain.

Bob had a bite to eat with his wife Barbara who then needed to run an errand. He told her before she left that he was not feeling good and she promised to be back soon and encouraged him to rest. After eating his supper he decided just to sit there for a while at the kitchen table.

Back in Alabama, I showered and pulled out a copy of John Grisham's The Client. I loved to wind down my day with a great book. Grisham is a talented author and a great source of inspiration to me. I often imagined if I had continued to pursue creative writing in college or even stayed with communications, I might be closer to realizing my dream of being a successful writer like Grisham. With my business degree, I could go back to school, maybe law school just like Grisham and perhaps then become a Novelist.

While I curled up on the couch in my trailer and entered a fantasyland of daydreaming and reading, Bob laid his head across his kitchen table and went to sleep for the very last time. Barbara came home to find him slumped over the table, dead.

At 11 PM my mother knocked on my door. When I opened the door she was standing there white as a ghost. She didn't sugar coat, she didn't hedge, "Wormy called. Bob died of a heart attack." I didn't know what to say. It didn't matter that I wasn't ready for this to happen. It didn't matter that I thought my entire life that one day we would mend fences and have a relationship. It no longer mattered that I had fantasized about one day impressing Bob Gowens so much that he would run to me, hat in hand and apologize, ask for a relationship with me and that Ona Lee would support or even encourage it. The sand ran out on the hourglass. Time was up. I could sing "daddy don't go" as many times as I wanted, but he was gone forever.

Ona Lee encouraged me to get dressed and she would drive with me to Hokes Bluff to be with my Granny Gowens. When we arrived at the brick home on US Highway 278, also known as the Piedmont-Gadsden Highway, Aunt Wormy and her younger brother Uncle Gary were there consoling my grandmother. We embraced, she told me how good I looked and I sat down beside her. They told me all the details they had heard and now we would just wait. We would wait for instructions from Barbara and the step-kids on when we would bury my biological father.

I drove back home with my mother about 6 AM, called my office to let them know what happened and called my Granny Cochran. She was devastated. She loved Bob Gowens even though she didn't approve of his ways. She and I both could not believe seven years had passed since I spoke to him. Seven years of college, a broken engagement, relocating and back again, the death of two close relatives, the beginning of a new career and no communication with him. He lost more of his eyesight, lost jobs, suffered pain and agony, but no communication with his one and only son. Now it was all over. I had no information or idea about his faith, yet I would stand over his coffin and mourn him as the only biological child he ever conceived.

I traveled back to the home where my father grew up to support Granny Gowens and to meet the rest of my Dad's family. I met my Uncle Glennis and Aunt Dene for the very first time. Uncle Glenn was retired from Alabama Power and held an MBA from the University of Alabama. He was just as impressed with me as I was with him. He apologized for never meeting me and for not reaching out to my mother all the years while I was growing up. "How could I not know you,' he kept asking. Aunt Wormy assured me that Uncle Glennis was hard to impress, but I had managed to do it in just a few hours. I was shocked at just what a wonderful family I had missed out on being part of. I was in a whirlwind of emotions.

We traveled to Carrollton for the funeral. The wake was to be held near Barbara's home then we would bring the body back to Alabama to buried in Lander's Cemetery beside Thurman Gowens.

I met relatives galore and felt a great deal of love. I was the center of attention and it was somewhat seductive. The family was nothing like my mother illustrated all those years as I was growing up. I began to understand that as a scorned woman she had a different view of her ex-husband's family. I felt the loss of so many years without knowing and loving this family the way I did the Cochran's and Goodwin's. I felt cheated.

At the funeral home, we sat in the sanctuary awaiting Barbara and her clan's arrival. My cousin Tammy and I were visiting and catching up on many years that had passed. I met Tammy as a little boy and spent some time with her and her Dad Gary, but we had been apart for years and I didn't have the closeness with them that I did with Aunt Wormy. Tammy looked behind us and saw Barbara walk into the chapel with her grown kids in tow. We stood up to greet them.

Barbara stopped and hugged Tammy and then nodded to me, "Tammy, this must be your husband?" Tammy nearly fainted and replied "I beg your pardon, Barbara, are you telling me you don't know him?" I put my hand out and introduced myself. Immediately Barbara grabbed me and began hugging the life out of me. She squeezed and squeezed my back into her chest, calling me Robby. "I have dreamed about this day. We love you so much, we have your pictures all over our house," she explained. Tammy interrupted with a firm tone, "Really Barbara? Pictures all over the house but you didn't know who he was?"

The next two days were a dance between Barbara, her clan and me. They doted on me, begged me to make plans to visit, offered to fill me in on every aspect of my father's life. Aunt Wormy was livid. She, Uncle Gary, and Uncle Glennis kept interrupting them and pulling me away each time they tried to engage with me. Bob's siblings were adamant that Barbara had kept Bob away from the family and me. I'll never know the truth, honestly he is the only one who really knows why he made the decisions he made, so I don't blame Barbara or her family. She was kind to me, but it did seem too little and definitely it was too late.

We laid Robert T. Gowens to rest on September 25, 1997. He was given a military burial for his service in the Army. He was honorably discharged while serving in Germany and awarded a purple heart. The sergeant folded a beautiful American flag and walked to Barbara to place it in her lap, but she handed it to Granny Gowens who placed it in my lap. I am forever grateful and I treasure it.

I held up well during the funeral, but afterwards, the culmination of every emotion I have ever known regarding Daddy Bob erupted and I fell apart. I made it to Bertie Mae's swing and together we wept for days.

CHAPTER TWELVE

Depression is ugly. It is a terrible demon. This is not a disease that can be repaired with surgery or a simple prescription. Mental illness is certainly manageable depending on the patient, but when you are in the midst of a major manic cycle and you don't even realize what it is that you have, there is nothing simple or hopeful about treatment. Upon the advice of a friend, I made a visit to a doctor. A prescription for Zoloft was given, I was patted on the back and sent on my way. It didn't work.

Just as it had since I was five years old, Bipolar Disorder manifested itself in every aspect of my life. I became a relentless overachiever at my job and a depressed and sad lunatic at home. During the day I could conquer the world and at night, I could conquer a bottle of vodka, hiding in my closet with any spare towel, blanket, shirt whatever I could find to stuff around the door and hide any glimmer of light from the outside world. I literally crave darkness when I am manic. It's my way of hiding.

If no light can make its way into a room then no one can see me. That's my rationale; just hide from everyone around me and maybe I won't even know what's going on. Depression affects each person individually but the pain exists and it is dangerous. Unreported feelings of worthlessness, thoughts of suicide, hopelessness, etc. is not something anyone can live with for long without hitting rock bottom. I decided to climb just as far as I could so the fall would be much worse, silly impulsive me!

The spring of 1998 I became a well-known figure in my business community after capturing a local public speaking competition title. Through my work with the Alabama Jaycees I had the opportunity to travel to Dothan in South Alabama to compete for the state public speaking championship.

Sponsored by the Glencoe Jaycees I cultivated a community outreach program against violence in schools and utilized it as my platform for the state competition. Through my interview process and eventual eight minute prepared speech I felt very confident. The previous year, before my father's death I competed and became a top 6 finalist, this year I was determined to make the final 3 in the state.

I delivered my speech before a panel of six professional judges and was not surprised when I made the top group of finalists once again and entered a second day of impromptu speeches. My friends and some colleagues traveled to Dothan to support me. My family was not able to attend and my mother was secretly hoping that I didn't win the all expense paid trip to Washington, D.C. for the national competition. She had always feared airplanes and never wanted me to fly. "I have had a recurring dream that you died in a plane crash," she always told me. Mom has always been excellent with scare tactics. Fortunately they don't work on grown folks very often.

I was overjoyed and soaring high in the clouds on the final night when I was announced as the 1998 Alabama Public Speaking Champion. This was a huge accomplishment and the awards ceremony was something really special. It truly fed my narcissistic needs and kept me on an upswing of emotions for months. I could do anything! The local papers ran stories about my victory and commitment to community service and my employer held a special event in my honor.

A few months later I got on that plane much to the dismay of my mother and flew to our nation's capital to make my mark. I represented the state of Alabama at the national event emceed by former Miss America Kaye Lani Rafko. I continued to utilize my platform of "Don't Act Out, Reach Out." The Columbine shooting occurred the spring of 1999 and was a prominent topic in D.C. Senator Ted Kennedy was one of the judges and I had the pleasure of meeting the famous Democrat from Massachusetts.

There were four attorneys and two legislative speechwriters who represented their states in the competition, but none of them made the top ten finalists, but I did. I was ecstatic to call home and let my mother and Bertie Mae know that I was the first contestant from Alabama to make the top ten in the competitions twelve-year history. I embraced the impromptu round and began to daydream about what it would be like to win the national competition and travel to Niagra Falls for the International Public Speaking Championships. On the final day, I received the award for Second Runner-Up and an automatic bid with the Winner (Tennessee) and First Runner-Up (Ohio) to Canada for the Internationals. Finishing in the top 3 in the United States in Public Speaking was a major accomplishment.

The downside to accomplishing something so extraordinary is exactly just that, the coming down from it, the sobering effect if you will. By the time I got home, I was the saddest person on earth. I had absolutely no idea how to control my emotions. Was I soaring too high and making too big of a deal out of my career? I didn't understand being so happy on one hand and crying uncontrollably on the other. In the coming months, this would be my life, crazy highs and the lowest of lows.

I gained 10 lbs. one week and lost 10 the next. I purchased hundreds and hundreds of dollars of clothing and never removed the tag. I became impulsive with every single aspect of my life. I became careless, promiscuous, sedentary, and defiant. Bipolar Disorder can cause so much self-destruction and harm the lives of a family. For the first time, I realized how out of control I really was and I looked back on the fact that I didn't marry Sonja with relief. I can't imagine dragging a wife and child through the ups and downs I was facing.

My promotions at work just kept coming and I now was on a different airplane every day covering the entire East Coast Division. I would fly to Richmond one day to roll out a new marketing campaign, leave that evening for Tampa, and the next day be in Atlanta to negotiate a new agreement with franchise owners. I was a jet-setter and it was glamorous, but I was so impulsive.

I drove to Michigan in one weekend to look for a house to buy and I had never even been to Michigan and no business there. My company was not there. It was simply an impulse and one that I couldn't control. I needed help and I just didn't know where to find it. I tried relying on spiritual guidance from my local congregation, but that didn't turn out well. I was convinced to quit my job, take a position within the ministry, and it didn't last even nine months. I became erratic and undependable. I came very close to destroying my career with wildly inappropriate decisions and I hid everything from my family and loved ones. This is called mania and it is dangerous!

By the age of 30 I felt as though I had no feelings left in my body for anyone other than Bertie Mae and her health was declining rapidly. At 93 years old we were not seeing each other as much as we wanted to, I was always traveling and she was feeling that I had deserted her. I slipped further and further away from my faith. This thing, this depression that I was feeling caused me to nearly lose my salvation. It truly had me in a state of mind where I didn't think God loved me or would ever help me again. I couldn't pinpoint the cause. I didn't feel like I was in mourning, I just felt completely out of control of my own mind and body.

Growing up in a conservative and legalistic faith, the talk of mental health was forbidden. People who read this and knew me then may disagree, but I witnessed good strong Christian women and men being exiled and blacklisted from the church because of mental disorders. Those same Elders at the church where I grew up who claim to be Godly Shepherds would sit in small groups and talk about the women who were on Prozac and other antidepressants and claim they were weak in their faith. *Depression is not a result of weak faith, but it did cause me to grow weak in my faith.* Once again, the weakness of faith for me came as a result of depression, not depression as a result of poor faith. I was doing everything I knew to do to serve God. I was a youth minister and I used my creative talents to benefit the Church. What I suffer from is a mental illness and it attacks the very foundation of my capacity to control behavior and moods. Every person reacts differently, but I felt so judged for behavior that I never understood the whys of its manifestation. Just like the medical community was slow to acknowledge depression in children, the Church was even slower to recognize and accurately assist its members.

We admonish each other constantly about judgment. "Thou shalt not judge," a person may say. "Those who live in glass houses should not throw stones," is another phrase we use on each other, however, do we really practice what we preach? Sometimes I think as Christians we are much more destructive when we preach things we cannot possibly practice ourselves. We set expectations for others that we can't possibly conform to in our own walks with Jesus.

I impulsively made another career change and found myself living in a wooded cabin on Lake Wedowee seventy miles south of Jacksonville. It was the worst decision that I have ever made because removing myself from family and friends was not something I could ever mentally handle. I know that Bertie Mae had no idea how to help me. I know that she just remained steadfast in prayer and trusted that the Lord would find a way for me to find better mental health.

I hid as much as I could from those who loved me, but the look in Bertie Mae's eyes proved that she knew I was suffering and that I was on a destructive path to end my own life. Her conversations with me became very soft spoken and tired.

Bertie Mae set a goal years earlier that she wanted to live to be 100. *On The Today Show* if you reached 100 you got your name mentioned in a commercial and you received a birthday card from the President of the United States. Strong in her independence, Bertie Mae remained in her own home even thought her health started to decline in the early 2000's.

In the fall of 2003 I took few days off work and came home to visit. Bertie Mae and I sat in her living room and watched a few episodes of The Waltons someone recorded for her and we talked about my mood swings. "You have been a different kind of fellow all your life, Sugar," she said to me. "It doesn't matter, being different from other people is the way you should be. You just have to find out what it is that God wants to do with your life." I have heard that explanation about our individual relationships with God all of my life and it is hard to comprehend at times. God doesn't exactly call us on the phone or write us a personal letter to tell us what he expects from us. It is honestly something that you can't understand until you finally really know what it is. Realizing your place in this world and your spiritual role in the kingdom of God can come at different times for different folks, just like every other accomplishment in life. It takes patience and we all know patience is a virtue.

That last full day that I spent with my Bertie Mae, I just couldn't get enough of our conversation. I needed more of her wisdom and I didn't understand at that moment that all of my life she had really given me the foundation to go out and do whatever I needed to do and conquer even the worst life had to offer, which for me is mental illness.

Granny kept a bookshelf next to her bed with photos of all of her children, grandchildren, great-grandchildren, and even great great-grandchildren. She was a lover of photos. In it's original envelope, she also kept the photos I had developed for her of our trip to the beach back in 1994. We looked at those photos again that day and talked about those walks we had. She reminded me that one day we were going to walk the shores of Heaven together and I agreed but reminded her she was going to make it to 100.

CHAPTER THIRTEEN

People of different walks of life have varying traditions. What one family considers a priority or a must may not be the same to another. In the Cochran family anytime there has been an illness or approaching death, the entire family is present. We all have our own sets of friends and people we would rather spend time with than one another, but when a crisis approaches, we come together and we support one another the best that we know how. We sit up all hours of the night, crying together, laughing and reminiscing, arguing and worrying. In my generation of Cochran cousins we unfortunately accustomed to losing loved ones and bond together during someone's final goodbye.

Bertie Mae was our matriarch. She survived the death of her parents, siblings, aunts and uncles, her husband, and recent death of her middle son Charles. She held her children and grandchildren in her arms as they said goodbye to parents and siblings. She saw more than her share of death and tragedy in the ninety-four years eleven months and six days of her life. She also knew great victory and triumph. She had a wonderful relationship with Jesus Christ and set an example for several generations.

In October of 2003 my cousins and I gathered to support our parents, aunts and uncles and each other as we let go of our angel, Bertie Mae. We were blessed as the Lord allowed us to say goodbye just the way we would have wanted and allow her to drift away after making sure we were all okay. A massive spike in her sugar sent Bertie Mae to the hospital on Monday morning. I got the call and rushed to her side in Jacksonville.

Granny was drifting in and out of consciousness when I arrived, but she knew me. I held her hands and caressed her skin. I gazed into her eyes and saw the many colors. I played with the Citrine stone ring I had given her a few November's ago. She knew that I was there and that was all that mattered to me at the moment.

Throughout the day there were ups and downs and the news was grim. It was obvious we were close to the end and even though I had lamented this day for many years, I felt a sense of peace on that day. Some family members were more emotional than others. Some were in denial and others in shock. Bertie Mae was just one of those characters that no one could ever imagine dying. She had beaten the odds so many times and had a mind that was as sharp as the day any of us met her. Friends from the Church poured in and out all day offering love and support. We were all moved and appreciative.

As evening approached our strong Granny grew weak. She suffered back-to-back heart attacks and we were told there were only a few moments left, but I was quiet, I knew differently. She was not quite finished just yet. She had another lap or two in her. Doctors were once again amazed by her strength as she awoke and sat up in the bed. She talked with all of us, visited with brethren, and was even able to laugh a little. The nurses assigned to her case were stunned and amazed. Her life had been a testimony and so was her death.

She asked me if I was okay and if I remembered what we had talked about when this moment came. I agreed and told her that I had been preparing all of my life. I knew that I would need a little help from God and a brother in Christ, but yes, I could do it, I could preach her funeral.

Most of us stayed the night at the hospital and in the wee hours of the morning, the heart attacks began again. Her sugar was spiking, her kidneys were shutting down, and she was in great pain. There was no calming her down with words. My mother and her sisters were distraught and crying uncontrollably, too upset to interact with the nurses. The nursing supervisor took me by the hand and led me around the corner. She told me that Granny was in great pain. "She's actually having heart attacks and it is very painful for her," she explained.

Obviously Bertie Mae at the age of 94 was considered DNR, so no activity to save her could take place, but the nurse offered a small dose of morphine to help her to calm and ease the pain she was in. "She's going," she told me, "we need to help her to relax." A couple of my cousins and my Uncle were standing in the room and we agreed as the nurse gave her the morphine. She began to relax and it was almost over. I stood at the head of her bed and I cradled her in my arms. I could barely form the words, but I whispered in her ear just seconds before the heart monitor sounded, "I'll see you at the beach," and I surely will.

I give all the glory to God for the life he gave Bertie Mae and that I got to be hers for 31 years of my life. I am honored to be her grandson and I am honored to tell you the story of her life and what her influence did after she was gone and is still doing today. Bertie Mae Duncan-Cochran was considered a treasure by all who knew her. She was the epitome of mercy, grace, and love. Every day she told someone about Jesus and her walk with Him.

Writing the eulogy for my grandmother was actually the easiest piece of work I have ever written. It flowed freely onto the paper just as the tears do when I miss her. People always say, write what you know about and I knew about her. I knew what she was thinking and I knew everything she wanted for each of us.

I didn't fall apart right away, because there was work to be done. I knew that my mother was devastated and would not know how to function in a world without Bertie Mae. She had her mother almost 60 years. A person loses the best friend they have ever known in life when they lose their mother. I felt pain for Emily and Myrtle, for Hoyt, and for Charles' surviving kids, Carl and Diane. She was everything for all of us. We each had a very special relationship with this angel.

I selected the preacher Scotty Sparks to assist me with the funeral. Scotty is married to Celine, the daughter of Bertie Mae's favorite niece Johnna. My cousin Sherry recorded Amazing Grace accapella to play during the service. We kept it in the family and it would be beautiful and just what Granny would have wanted. I knew, because I knew her.

I wanted to make sure the entire family was represented in the eulogy so my cousins and I gathered to share memories and include the special moments we wanted to recognize. I wanted to share the story of her life and what she meant to each of us as best I could. The Lord blessed me on the day of her funeral with the right way to say goodbye and articulate to our friends and loved ones just how special she was.

I stood at the lectern in front of a crowd of at least three hundred and began telling the beautiful story of a woman named Bertie Mae. We are truly blessed by God if we have an influence of someone like her in our lives. If we are lucky enough to ever know that kind of unconditional maternal love. Over the years as I have written about Granny and spoke of her lessons of love, more people have commented how it takes them back to the love they had for their grandparents or someone special in their life. A simple cotton-farming girl grew into a grand matriarch of a large southern family. We are neither wealthy nor influential. Our family is not especially educated or political. We are just a family of hard working, principled southerners. We do the best we can to keep the tradition of love and respect alive. We continue to share the bond she created in each of us. I want to do something in my life that will honor her. I am not ashamed or embarrassed to bring light to the subject of mental illness. Especially as a Christian I want to utilize the lessons and confidence she gave me to help my brothers and sisters in Him to recover and find their strength in faith once again.

I dreaded losing my best friend my entire life. From the moment I knew that I loved her, I wondered when she would leave me. Worry steals away the joy from life and I wish that I could trade a bushel of the worry for just a smidgen of the happiness I felt with her. I knew I had to go through this. I knew I had to hit my personal rock bottom before I could climb back to the top and truly flourish. We are never prepared to say goodbye, even when we know in our hearts it is only temporary.

God utilizes the people in our lives to keep us on the path we are destined to follow. Bertie Mae was the kind of woman who influenced many paths and was a resource for God in many lives, not just me. For me, she taught me about Jesus and how to secure my salvation through Him. She taught me how He is always there to pick us up and she gave me the strength to believe "The Lord's gonna take care of me." I feel like she and I had the bond so that I could survive the pain of depression and the obstacles in my future as well as my past. She loved me so that I could know the Lord and never leave Him for good. She was in my life to establish the firm foundation that as a child of God, I am a prodigal son and I can always return to Him.

When a loved one is buried there is always some form of closure. The realization that life goes on and we have to return to our jobs and our daily responsibilities is unavoidable. It's normal to be sad and in mourning for varying amounts of time depending on who we lose. My family was greatly concerned at just how I would deal with the loss. There was no secret about my emotions and my bond with Bertie Mae. I put on a good face for my family and returned to my life and work.

Christians know the devil is always aware of our weaknesses. Satan loves to kick a Christian when they are down and it was inevitable for me to be attacked during this time of great sorrow. I was an easy target. My depression already had me at a distance from my faith and I covered it with excuses, but now there was no way I could recover or battle without divine intervention. I was a sitting duck and I even feared my own self.

I am no doctor, and everyone is different in how they relate/react to their own conditions, but being alone can't be healthy for anyone who suffers from depression. Sometimes solitude is unavoidable because a depressed or mentally ill person is difficult to live with. Mental illnesses destroy more than just the lives of the sick person. These cruel almost parasitic diseases impact more than just their hosts. Returning to Lake Wedowee was setting myself up for failure, but I did it anyway. I convinced my family that by returning to my life quickly I would be much better off.

One week after Bertie Mae's death a good friend of mine, Chris Smith and I were hanging out on a Sunday and he suggested that we ride bikes. The Ladiga Bike Trail was formed from Weaver, AL and ran more than 25 miles to the Georgia state line. The old train rail had been transformed and would eventually connect with Georgia's Silver Comet Trail in Cedartown. Chris and I enjoyed getting out and doing things in the fall weather so we drove up to Weaver and hopped on the trail.

I have always been taught the devil can't know what we are thinking but he is powerful enough to put thoughts in our head. On that bike ride, I still felt the hollowness and sinking feeling of loss deep in my gut. My thoughts became more rapid and destructive and on that bike ride I created my way out. I began to think of a great plan to end my life so that I could be with Granny. I thought I was outsmarting God and that He wouldn't listen to these deep dark thoughts that had always lingered in my mind. If I could just make it look like an accident, I could easily fool my family, friends, coworkers and maybe even my Heavenly Father. Mental illness plays silly tricks on our minds especially when we think we can hide from God or deceive Him with personal thoughts.

I foolishly developed a creative plan, but I soon found out who was really in charge of my life.

CHAPTER FOURTEEN

I think there is a definite fine line between "being in your right mind" and not when it comes to depression. Friends and associates who have experienced similar symptoms as I confirm that in the midst of a cycle of depression clear thinking is almost impossible. I had everything in the world to live for. I was once again climbing a corporate ladder, enjoying many old and new friends, and I had a wonderful little boy in my nephew Austin who looked up to me as a father figure. There were plenty of reasons for me to embrace life, deal with my grief over losing Granny Cochran, and move on with my journey positively. Depression alters every sense a man has. Depression takes the rationale out of thinking.

My outer appearance has always been conservative. It always mattered to me what the perception of others was. I've been able to "disguise" my inner ugliness. I spent many years confused that my salvation depended on the views of the Church, rather than the Head of the Church, Christ. Jesus had the capacity to do more than any man ever could. He had the strength and willpower to suffer an agonizing death on the cross. He also has the ability to forgive like no man can. Once we realize that as a Christian, our life can become so much less stressful. When we stop trying to impress the couple on the second pew or some false teacher behind a podium, we learn to enjoy our own personal relationship with God. I was not at that place just yet in the months and years after Granny's death. I should have been, but all of her lessons hadn't sank in. I had not experienced the ah-ha moment of life.

My family did everything they possibly could do to keep me motivated and make sure that I was okay. I lied to my parents and to my closest cousin Sherry, who had grown up like a twin sister to me. She and I always experience a sixth sense about one another. When she hurts I hurt, and vice versa. There is no end to the list of people who reached out to see if I needed anything in that secluded little cabin.

I was fortunate to have a wonderful relationship with my supervisor Betty Hamrick. I knew Betty for a number of years and she watched me grow as a manager and leader. Betty could tell more than any other person who interacted with me daily that things were not right. She was a great listener.

In the house on Lake Wedowee I had more room than any one person could ever need. There were four bedrooms and four bathrooms in the two level cottage built overlooking the backwater off Old Alabama Highway 431. The upper or main level had a large deck and beautiful views, but I rarely enjoyed it because I wanted to hide inside away from the world and away from God. I shopped at a local thrift store and purchased heavy blankets to cover all the windows. During my rapid cycling I would become obsessed with keeping light out of the house. My last resort to escape the light would be to hide in a hall closet and place towels along the bottom of the door to block any light.

In that closet I would call Betty. "You talk and I will listen," I would explain with my voice shaking and she always would. She used to tell me that she didn't know how to help me, but everything she did was a help to me. She wasn't my immediate family and I could be raw with her. I could just feel my pain and know that she was on the other line serving as a life raft for sanity.

Chris Smith continued to encourage me to ride bikes and hike with him. He was incredibly athletic and truly enjoyed the outdoors. He also thought he was helping his friend by inviting him to do active outings and occupy my mind. I used this opportunity to create the ultimate plan to end my life. I had never been known as an athletic dude, so there would be no question that I just got out of my element if I accidentally rode my bike off the side of Cheaha Mountain.

Chris and I continued to train on smaller trails in White Plains and Heflin. We hiked the larger and more treacherous routes along the mountain to build our leg strength. Occasionally we would come upon a large cliff like the one at Bald Rock. The view was beautiful and the drop off was intimidating. I could have spontaneously slipped, fallen, or jumped, but I didn't. The timing had to be just right and the loose ends of my life needed to be tied up.

I increased my life insurance policy and added an accidental rider. I wanted to make sure that my mother had the money she needed to secure their future, provide for Austin and take care of my final arrangements. If my death was ruled an accident, the insurance would double and even though money would not replace me it would certainly make life easier for my mother and Daddy Floyd. I realize just how selfish I was. I still am at times. Depression makes a person extremely selfish and narcissistic because we cannot see past our own issues and feelings, especially if there is no treatment plan.

Half-heartedly I worshiped at the Weaver Church of Christ after Granny's death. C.E. Chappell and his lovely wife Jean were my Ministers and very good friends. I met them years earlier at the Jacksonville congregation and they both had a deep love for Bertie Mae and she for them. Jean would visit Granny and bring her egg custards. Those desserts reminded Bertie Mae of a dish her mother made growing up and it warmed her soul. Jean and C.E. were the most generous people I have ever known. They were generous with their time, love and resources.

Jean Chappell would be proud to be called a busy body. If you were in her circle and suddenly became absent, she was determined to find you. I really didn't understand exactly why she was that way at the time, but it perturbed me a bit. I gave every excuse I could think of as to why I was missing Sunday services. I slipped further into my seclusion and began ignoring phone calls, emails and all forms of communication from my loved ones.

Oxford, Alabama is about half the distance between Lake Wedowee and my home in Jacksonville. It is a growing town that sprawls across interstate 20 between Atlanta and Birmingham and is a major retail hub for several counties in northeast Alabama. I found a little bike store on Snow Street with a sale on Cannondale mountain bikes. If I was going to look like a mountain biker then I certainly needed something a little better than the cheap Wal-Mart bike I had purchased for training with Chris.

I bought a 2004 Cannondale that only weighed 24 lbs. It would be perfect for climbing trails. I kept thinking that when I finally reached that point where I couldn't stand life anymore, I would just take my last ride and would go down in the history of my family as another tragic death. There would be respect in my death. The fellow Christians would stand and say, "oh he is in Heaven now with Bertie Mae." Of course in my deluded mind it only mattered how others judged me, I was not thinking about God, His plan for me, or the jeopardy I would be putting my salvation in.

To realize the instability of my thinking at the time, you have to understand just how much guilt and regret I felt. Self-pity loves the company of more self-pity. What maybe started out as missing my grandmother manifested into the analyzing of every decision I ever made. I went back to the days when I chose Goodwin over Gowens and watched Daddy Bob walk out of my life. I concentrated on violence that occurred when my mother and Daddy Floyd fought each other physically. I obsessed about what made Becky run away from home at 18 and how deep dark secrets in my own life kept me from appreciating her struggles. I was selfish. I mistreated Sonja and lost my one chance at being a husband and father. I felt that I had squandered my opportunities after winning the speaking competitions and would never realize true success or career fulfillment again. Yes, pity loves pity and often parties in great numbers.

The week that was to be the final week in the life of Robert C. Goodwin I spent time crossing all my T's and dotting my I's. I drove to Jacksonville and to the outskirts of town along the cotton fields to the cemetery where Bertie Mae was buried. I sat on the cinderblock wall that encompassed the graves of Bertie Mae, J.D. and Luther. I talked out loud to Granny and to God. I wept and apologized for the disappointment that I had become. I sank deeper into the uncontrolled state of sadness and grief. There was no way I was snapping out of this mindset without some kind of divine intervention. I was at the lowest of lows. *It was rock bottom*

I have never had a personal relationship with anyone who committed suicide. I have heard rumors that this person did or that person might have, but I was never motivated by an example set by someone else. No one in my family repeatedly bragged or threatened that they could or would take their own lives. In fits of anger, I heard my parents at times threaten to harm each other, but never themselves. I wasn't a stranger to violence, but I also was not an active participant. I never read any books on suicide or felt that it had been sensationalized for me by some movie or famous actor's death. I had no feeling about the act of suicide other than it being the only way to escape the torture of my own mind. That is it in a nutshell, living in my head is sometimes torturous and I had no idea how to fix that. I tried going the medical route and within three minutes of talking with a doctor a prescription was being written and it only made me feel worse.

I am a wise and educated man, yet all of these years I didn't have the common sense or discipline to search out help for the way I was feeling. To wrapped up in my own sorrow, self-pity and instability to ask for help, that's what kind of man I became. It makes me wonder just how many people, especially men, go down that way? *How often are we too concerned with how others will view our treatment to seek help?* The act of admitting a problem can be just as bad as having the issue.

Chris and I made plans for Saturday. We pinpointed the trails and thought we were ready to tackle some of the rougher routes. I hated to do it to him, but I needed confirmation that it was an accident. I needed him to confirm that I was in good spirits that day and we were just carrying out a normal bike ride as part of our training to be healthier men in their thirties. Chris would be my alibi for the family, friends and God.

I packed up liquor bottles and anything else that I didn't want my parents to know about and took it to the Randolph County dump. I caught up all my administrative duties for work and organized my files. I wanted this to be as peaceful as possible for my mother, but how could it be? I was selfish, selfish, and selfish. Thursday approached and I retired to my bed thinking about what would occur in forty-eight hours. You know how they say that God never puts more on us than we can handle? He showed me that night exactly how He works.

CHAPTER FIFTEEN

I dream vividly. A state of sleep for me includes a whirlwind of colorful, frightening, exciting, joyful, traumatic, and downright crazy dreams. My imagination has always carried over into my dreams to the point that relatives have even asked me "did you just dream that," when I am retelling some outrageous occurrence in my life.

Thursday evening before my planned Saturday suicide I fell asleep with the small box fan running beside my bed. I had gone through my normal routine of double-checking the locks on all the doors, turning out the lights, and setting my alarm clock. Somewhere in the subconscious of my sleep I heard a knock at my door. In reality, I would have slept through that knock considering the distance between my master bedroom and the front door. This was a dream though, so I was just going to roll with it.

Over the years I have had such colorful and recurring dreams I can remember them for years. This is one for the ages for sure. I stumbled to my front door and opened it to see my Bertie Mae standing there. She wore a beautiful floral dress that fell just below her knees. There was no apron around her waste however. I hugged her as tightly as possible and I could even smell the unmistakable tones of her skin and hair. I am not sure what our initial conversation was but in my dream we ended up seated on my couch next to the fireplace. In the dream, the fireplace was lit, but this wasn't part of reality because it was late spring and rather warm.

The look in Granny's eyes let me know that she knew what I was up to. There was no hiding it. She had been watching me or had heard my pleas. I immediately felt a sensation that she was here to save me from my own hand. She told me how much she loved me and was looking forward to being with me again, but it was not time. It would be a while before the time would come. I begged her to stay with me, to return to my dreams each night and talk with me. If she would just do that, I could make it. I could survive each day. I had so much to tell her that I had hidden deep inside for years. I felt like I was talking twice as fast as normal, just trying to get the words in before I was disturbed in my sleep. I wanted to confess so much. I wanted her to know all the things I was hiding, even darker things that had happened or haunted me.

We held hands and she told me that I would find the help that I needed. She encouraged me to remember all of our conversations and prayers together in the porch swing. Just like when I was a little boy, she reminded me to apply the lessons I learned in Sunday school. I confessed to her that I was not in church right now and that I felt I had fallen away. She told me it would all be changing soon. I wanted to sit there with her forever because it seemed so very real. I could touch her, hear her, and smell her. I wanted to go with her. "Just let me go now, here in my sleep," I begged. I was selfish again and I had to listen to the words and process "it's not time."

Almost as quickly as she came in my dream she was gone. I rolled on my back, snored and startled myself to full consciousness. I sat up in the bed and looked around at the dark room with only a small glimmer of moonlight coming through the blinds. I threw my legs across the edge of the bed placing my feet on the floor and gently stood. I made a quick trip to the restroom and then ventured down the hall to grab a swig of some cold Sprite I left in a can in the refrigerator. I was stunned to find my front door standing wide open. I was not afraid at all. I felt grateful for the experience to talk with Granny. There are probably five or six different scenarios that I could imagine as to how the door got opened, but I choose to just let it be my own little miracle.

The visit from Granny didn't convince me to cancel my destructive plans for Saturday. It made me think about it, but I was still sleepy and just told myself that I would give it more thought in the morning. I passed my office on the way back to the bedroom and noticed my answering machine blinking. I had turned in shortly before 9 PM so someone must have called after I drifted into my sleep. I pressed play and the message of Jean Chappell broadcasted loudly through the room, I was surprised it had not woken me when she recorded it. "Rob Goodwin, this is Jean Chappell," she commanded. "You have not been to church and you have not returned my phone calls. C.E. and I want to hear from you young man. We need to talk. Young man, we love you. Call me." I deleted the message and went back to bed.

When the early hours of the morning arrived and the sun began to peer through, the sound of knocking on my front door awoke me again. Was this sound part of another dream? I grabbed my shower robe this time and headed down the hallway as I tied it around my waist. I opened the glass door to see Jean and C.E. Chappell standing on my front stoop. There was not much of a greeting, they just walked right past me into the foyer and toward my living room. Jean was very polite, but she was on a mission.

I made a pot of coffee and began to cultivate excuses in my mind to explain my absences from service so I could get these lovely people on their way. I had one more day of work to get to and I needed to get moving. Jean had other plans. She launched into her own personal story of depression. She told me about the first time she was diagnosed with breast cancer in the early 1990s and how she had laid her head in C.E.'s lap and cried for hours even after going into remission. She felt hopeless and less of a person. She planned to drive her car over a cliff and had chosen the exact spot and time. Her daughter Karen was an adult and married, C.E. could find another wife near where he worked in Montgomery, and she would be out of her misery. I recognized the feelings she described, but kept my guard up.

"Depression is like someone throwing a wet blanket over you and you just can't find your way out," she explained. "Rob, you are depressed. We understand. We know it is a real disease. We know better than anyone and we are here to help you." It was not the words, it was the way she said it. The soft but authoritative tone which assured me she wouldn't take no for an answer. It was the dream from the night before about Granny. It was the beginning of a series of events that would give me that ultimate ah-ha moment about my individual relationship with God. It was our Heavenly Father saying to me, "you have had enough. You are at the point where you can't handle anymore alone." Oh my goodness….you have to know, you have to believe this was God. This was the median for me to turn around on this wrong highway of destruction I was traveling.

Within an hour I had called into my job and let them know I was in need of a sick day. I showered, got dressed and slid into the back of the Buick Roadmaster the Chappell's owned. C.E. drove us back roads and pig trails through Lineville, Sylacauga, into Montgomery and finally in Selma down in southwest, Alabama. I didn't understand why we had to travel this far for a doctor. Jean had visited a mental health clinic in Selma many years earlier and found the necessary guidance and assistance she needed. Jean and C.E. trusted the doctor they knew and felt it was a great step for my recovery.

I sat in a chair across from the doctor, who was seated behind her desk. I couldn't find the words so I just showed her a picture of my grandmother and began to shake and cry. This particular doctor of course thought I was suffering from simple grief and depression and although her diagnosis was not accurate, it was the beginning of finding a true diagnosis and it was the intervention I needed to cancel my Saturday plans.

After visiting the doctor, I slid back in the backseat of the car and Jean positioned herself right beside me. She placed a pillow on her lap and motioned for me to stretch out and lay my head on the pillow. "You brought this for me," I asked? She replied, "I thought you might just need it." On the long drive back to Wedowee I opened up and told them everything I had been experiencing, thinking, and lamenting. I talked about changing my name at five years old and about losing my father, hating and loving him at the same time. I talked about worrying about Granny's death my entire life and then not being prepared when it arrived. We talked about the beautiful eulogy I was able to deliver and how I crashed emotionally afterwards. The Chappells' made plans with me to follow up with a Psychiatrist close to home so that I could undergo more testing and find an accurate diagnosis. C.E. educated me spiritually about my condition and helped me figure out how to process the shame and embarrassment that I felt. He encouraged me to believe that depression affected millions of men and that I should not be one of the many who are defeated because of misplaced pride.

This intervention did not solve my problems by a long shot, but it was the first and most necessary step to anyone's recovery from a chronic mental illness. I had to admit to myself and to someone else there was a problem. By acknowledging what was going on to C.E. and Jean Chappell, accountability was assigned to me. I no longer could hide behind the "it will look like an accident," mentality. As a Christian this is what I had lost. I let go of my accountability to God and to those who loved me. I needed to rediscover a sense of belonging to someone else without judgment and I found that in C.E. and Jean.

The Chappell's were an amazing couple. C.E. taught for many years at Alabama Christian College. Jean was an executive secretary for the Chief of Staff for Governor George Wallace. They were a great example to me of sophistication, success, and faith. I found great comfort in sharing stories with Jean. She understood each feeling of helplessness and sorrow that I experienced. I recognized the symptoms she described and knew that if a Minister's wife could be open about her mental health, there was no reason that I couldn't.

My family was apprehensive and judgmental as a first reaction to the news that I was seeking medical help for depression. Only one other person in our family had ever sought this kind of help as publicly as I was about to and she was deemed "crazy." I had to toughen my resolve and embrace the "crazy" label for myself. My mother was extremely concerned about me, but often referred to my illness in the beginning as "your other little problem." Even in the middle 2000's in my circle mental health was not a prevalent topic. It needed to be brought to the forefront and I really didn't realize at the time that I was going to be the vehicle for this.

This would not be the last time I ever considered suicide, but I would never find myself planning the details and taking the steps to execute as I had done on this occasion. We are all at different places in our walk with Jesus. We all experience different levels of spirituality and faith, but for me, I crossed over to the place where I was willing to completely submit to God. I will always believe that God used Bertie Mae's memory to intervene in my sleep that night. The feeling deep within Jean and C.E. Chappell that they had to drive to Wedowee, an hour from their home that Friday morning was planted by God. I know this just as I know the sun will shine tomorrow. This was God!

Over the years I heard many Ministers speak about their calling to teach. Singers acknowledge their talent and give praise for a calling to sing. Each person possesses a gift or talent as part of God's amazing plan for their life and to further His kingdom. I didn't fully commit or believe these teachings until I realized that God was speaking directly to me about my burdens. Living in a tortured mind all those years now had a light at the end of the tunnel. Perhaps, the things I learned along this journey would make a difference in someone else's life. Perhaps talents given to me by God would actually be the best therapy I could ever know for my own recovery.

A judgmentally minded person will question others and God when they proclaim just how strongly He is working in their lives until that self-absorbed person has their own enlightening moment with God. Our Heavenly Father was not finished working on me or through me. He gave me a surge of strength through this experience to face even more tragic struggles right around the corner, but I became a champion for Him and this was just the starting line.

CHAPTER SIXTEEN

Ronda Reeves, Betty Hamrick and Carla Grego truly pushed me to succeed and overcome my emotional struggles. I rarely confided in anyone at work, but fighting a battle with depression can become very difficult to hide. Carla was just a couple of years older than me and even though she couldn't relate to my particular situation, she recognized when there were changes in my moods. Occasionally my coworkers and I would travel and it was great to have someone like Carla or Betty nearby to listen when I needed them.

I wasn't known for being a passive or humble manager. My work ethic was strong and I held others to the same standards. After beginning some treatment for my depression I began to see a few mild changes in my personality on the job. I became more accepting of differences in people and more open to giving people a chance. A lovely middle-aged Hawaiian lady walked into one of my stores one day. She had no car and had just traveled on foot from a nearby Government housing complex. Leialoha Kaaihue smiled sweetly and asked if I was the manager and if I would consider talking with her about a job. As we chatted about her path from the Pacific to Alabama I was moved by how humble she was and willing to share the details of her life. She told me of issues that caused her to leave a home she loved and family she missed.

In rural Alabama, there was limited opportunity for an educated and experienced travel industry expert. She found it difficult to find someone to take a chance on her transferrable skills. I liked her and I saw a twinkle in her eye that let me know she was something special. Lei as I called her, started from the bottom and eventually climbed the ladder to the level that I was in when I hired her. She started her life completely over with no material possessions, even walking long distances in bad weather to work every single day. I saw her purchase her first vehicle and later a second. She moved into a larger home and enjoyed a prosperous career. By the time we both moved on from that area a significant influence had been made on each other's lives.

My experience with medical professionals during this healing process was as much of a roller coaster ride as my daily mood swings. I became so frustrated with doctors who wanted to pull out their prescription pad within ten minutes of meeting me. I knew that I didn't understand how to treat my condition, but I was smart enough to know I was given too many doses of different kinds of medicine and that part of my treatment plan shouldn't involve feeling this inhumane. Taking the wrong antidepressants for your condition can be lethal. Many patients have increased suicidal thoughts and tendencies with the wrong medication. I paid attention to my feelings and once again felt very accountable for my actions.

I remained quiet about my condition and treatment when talking with some of my family. My mother and Daddy Floyd were going through way too much strife on their own. Bertie Mae's death in 2003 came just one year after the death of Maw Maw Ruth Goodwin, Floyd Ray's mother. Then in the spring of 2004, Daddy was diagnosed with stomach cancer. My mother was devastated. She couldn't bare the thought of losing my stepdad just after losing her mother-in-law and mother. It was too much. I was fighting to bounce back from the manic episode after Bertie Mae's death and now we all needed to help Daddy fight. Without God's intervention, I would have given up after learning Daddy Floyd had cancer.

The best Physicians at The Kirkland Clinic in Birmingham advised us that surgery was not an option. The tumor was too massive and inoperable. Giving up was not an option for Ona Lee either. She encouraged me to help her find a specialized cancer program that could save his life. Daddy Floyd did not want to leave Austin, Tony, Becky, me, or Ona Lee. Floyd Ray loved family. His siblings were always around and supportive. They know how to be a great family. My Dad's sisters Doris, Irma, Barbara, and Mildred were particularly close and they remained firm that we would all fight hard.

The Cancer Centers of America is a group of specialized treatment hospitals for cancer patients. They typically see patients who have been sent home to die by other hospitals. I called their hotline and began a conversation with an intake representative named Chad. From the beginning it was clear this was an extraordinary facility. Each staff member we encountered throughout the process was amazing. Chad set the bar high in the beginning and it was exceeded time and again. The physicians were hopeful about the information we provided and our family was invited to Zion, Illinois for a consultation. Dad's insurance plan paid for 80% of any treatment from this facility, so we were willing to take on the remainder.

Tony and I made plans to travel with my parents who had never been on an airplane. Mother had barely traveled out of state and Dad was weak and tired. It would definitely be a challenge to transport them both I kept telling myself. The week before we were set to fly out, Ona Lee decided to clean out her cabinets and fell from a chair breaking her arm. She required immediate surgery. Daddy Floyd wanted to delay the trip for his wife to heal, but Ona Lee was determined that she could handle it and time was of the essence. We pressed forward with our plans.

My big brother and I loaded our parents into two wheel chairs and pushed them through the Birmingham airport toward our gate. We were to fly directly to Chicago where a car service would drive us the seventy-five miles north to Zion along the coast of Lake Michigan. I was nervous for my mother who had always panicked in the past when I flew with my job. She surprised me with her strength and willingness to do absolutely anything to save Floyd Ray.

Dr. Ingram, our family physician prescribed Xanax for my mother and she was very relaxed as the Southwest Boeing 727 lifted from the runway in Birmingham. Tony sat with our Dad and I with Ona Lee. I knew why she was fighting so hard. I recognized the worry lines on her face. This was all happening too soon. This getting older and losing your parents and seeing your kids endure tragedies and seeing your mate wilt away from cancer. She was not ready for any of it and the anguish was written all over her face. I realized my mother and I were both weak and strong at the same time. We were both just trying to hold onto our sanity.

The consultations went better than I expected as the doctors advised Floyd Ray remission was absolutely possible. They agreed that surgery was not yet an option, but aggressive treatments could shrink or even eradicate the tumor. It seemed to be a prognosis exactly opposite of what we heard in Birmingham. The downside was the requirement for the patient and a relative to remain in Zion, Illinois for three months and then return every thirty days thereafter. I had no idea how we were going to pull that off. We did have a wonderful family, but everyone worked and had lives to live. The expense of flying back and forth to Illinois and even funding a place to live there would be more than any of us were capable of providing. Faith stepped in and stomped the doubt.

My mother was able to rent an apartment for she and Daddy Floyd. She took FMLA from her position at Jacksonville State University. She accepted a position on the cleaning crew there when the cotton mill finally went out of business. Friends and coworkers donated PTO (paid-time-off) for my mother so that she could earn a paycheck while on her leave. Our family donated and raised money so that finances were never again a factor in this journey.

We developed the plan for Tony and I to return to Alabama and fly back in a month to visit. We rented Ona Lee a car and got them settled. The hospital offered affordable housing opportunities for its patients and family members. One of the hardest things I have ever done is to leave my parents in a strange city in Illinois. Tony literally had to drag me to the car when the time came for us to go to the airport. I had been an avid traveler for business, but the thought of my 60ish parents being away from home was a heavy burden. I just wanted to protect and care for them the way they had for me so many years. They were the two people holding my hand so many years ago when I was fighting for my life in the hospital and I hated to leave them.

Back home in Alabama I continued to battle my up and down emotions and seek treatment. The adrenaline of worry about my stepdad actually took much of the attention away from my own issues. During a manic episode I become a very narcissistic person and rarely am able to put anything about my life into perspective. Instead of hiding in a dark closet, I worked as much as possible to take care of things my mother needed. We coordinated with all the physicians and managed a schedule for travel back and forth that included my siblings, my mother and my Dad's sister Barbara. We were blessed that Aunt Barbara was willing to take time away from her job as a Realtor to help us travel with Daddy Floyd.

My parents were definitely softened by the birth of their grandson.
They dedicated their lives to helping him grow into a young man.
Floyd Ray, Ona Lee and Austin in one of their last photos together.

The treatment plan seemed to be going well. Floyd Ray was able to travel back home for the summer and only return every thirty days. He kept a strong appetite during his treatment and even enjoyed a fruitful garden. Floyd Ray, Ona Lee, my Aunt Doris and Uncle Buck worked together on the garden all summer. It was therapeutic, kept their minds occupied and their bodies active. Just before the winter of

2004/2005, the doctors announced that Floyd Ray was in remission. Local monitoring was required and after the New Year Dad would need to return to Zion for a new screening. We were extremely happy and relieved to hear this news.

Twenty-nine years had gone by since I stood beside Ona Lee and Floyd Ray at the Cleburne County Courthouse. Even though I was only three years old, I remember bits and pieces of that day. The two-tone Ford Gran Torino station wagon had a flat tire on our drive up Alabama Highway 9. Floyd Ray changed the tire in his suit and had us on our way in no time. Standing there beside my mother and stepfather to be I remember the Justice of The Peace leading us in a prayer. He advised all three of us to close our eyes and bow our heads. I closed my eyes and so that meant I got married too! It was a running joke in our family for many years. Floyd Ray and I talked about that day on one of our trips back to Illinois. We sat on a park bench overlooking Lake Michigan just across the Wisconsin state line in Kenosha. It was a beautiful sunny day and I was grateful to have that moment of reflection with the man who did his very best to fill a void in my life.

Christmas came out of nowhere that year and we were all so drained and emotionally exhausted. On Christmas Eve I watched Ona Lee and Floyd Ray dance around the living room like two young lovebirds and I was grateful for the change in their relationship and optimistic about his recovery. Unfortunately, our lives once again changed overnight. Christmas Day was very difficult for my Dad and he could barely stand. It was obvious that he needed to go to the ER, receive fluids and monitor his vitals. He kept pushing himself to wait until after Christmas to leave the house again, but there was no denying he was declining rapidly. We returned to the Jacksonville Hospital ER and of course he was admitted.

The treatment for cancer alone is enough to kill a healthy person let alone someone who had a massive tumor growing inside them. Our optimism and positive outlook came to a screeching halt that week as we watched Daddy Floyd wilt away from a staph infection. I desperately attempted to reach the doctors in Illinois who had given us so much hope, but there was no way Floyd Ray could make the trip in his condition. We had no choice but to wait. On Sunday morning the doctors told us his organs were shutting down and we called our family members to join us at his bedside. He asked for a moment with each of us and I will never forget the last words he spoke to me. I held his hand and watched his eyes swell with tears. "Son, I need you to take over now," he uttered. I could barely breathe. I was his middle son, his stepson, but not really, I was just as much his child as Tony or Becky. I gripped his hand, kissed his cheek and whispered "I closed my eyes too Daddy."

CHAPTER SEVENTEEN

There was only sixteen months between Bertie Mae and Floyd Ray's death. In that time, I felt that I had aged twenty years. Initially my Dad's death was not as difficult for me as losing Bertie Mae. My worry shifted from my own personal feelings of grief to that of my mother and Austin. I wondered how in the world they would function without him. Ona Lee and Floyd Ray's thirty-year marriage ended so tragically. There was a great deal of tumult between them when my sister, step-brother and I were growing up, but that had long since passed and Austin truly gave them a new lease on life and love. I realized now more than ever I would be battling my own depression and a heavy dose for my mother as well.

I dressed in my best black suit on January 8, 2005 and stood before 150 or so of our closest family and friends at the K.L. Brown Funeral Home in Jacksonville, just where I had stood bidding goodbye to Bertie Mae in October of 2003. I told stories of Floyd Ray's love for Alabama football. If Alabama lost on a cold fall Saturday, I would cry myself to sleep that night as my Dad paced the hall of our trailer cursing under his breath at whichever player, *or referee* caused us to lose the game. I was in awe of his knowledge of football. He wanted to play as a young kid, but broke his leg, spent way too much time in a cast and saw his growth stunted. Except for that, he would have made a great player.

Floyd Ray enjoyed life and was known in our family for a special relationship. The kind of love where he could find himself wound tightly around a small finger. It was my sister Becky. As we were growing up, she was Daddy's little girl. Becky could do no wrong and all she wanted to do was spend time with our Dad. During the summers Dad was home with us in the mornings and worked in the afternoons. When it came time for Daddy Floyd to leave for work, Becky would throw a hissy fit. She would wrap her arms tightly around his legs and prevent him from getting out of the house. She begged him to drive her up the street in the car and bring her back before he could leave and every single day he obliged. Granny was ready to switch her for fear she would make Floyd Ray late for the shift at the mill.

Austin had almost as much pull with his granddad as my sister did, but I was there through both and I knew he had no greater love than what he felt for Becky. I knew that she would have regrets and would miss him for a very long time. I felt the same and I suspect so did Tony.

The Cochran family took major hits in 2005 because of this terrible disease called cancer. My eldest first cousin Eddie Cochran died that summer at the young age of 49. Only six months later, Myrtle's longtime husband Noble Lane also lost his battle with cancer and our family once again buried three close loved ones in a calendar year.

I continued to separate my depression from work and my family as much as possible. I never felt comfortable sharing with my mother just how significant and dangerous my condition had become because she was dealing with so much grief on her own. I confided in C.E. and Jean Chappell and other friends from church. I was fast approaching another breaking point where I had to make necessary changes in my life.

My mother's sister Emily and I became even closer the older I got. I found it easier to talk to her and share secret pain that I was dealing with. She has an open mind about mental health and I can always count on her to shoot straight with me. Emily knew that two really important things were wrong in my life. I was not faithfully committed to a congregation and I was living alone in the woods of Lake Wedowee. "You need to get out of those woods, it's not good for you Rob," she would say to me over and over. "I also think you need to get back in church," she explained.

I had to dwell on the last statement a bit because Emily is a godly woman but she is not interested in organized religion. She did not attend church with me, but she knew how important worship service had always been with me and with Bertie Mae. She knew that I missed it and it was missing in my life. I really applaud her for being able to recognize that in me. I used to try and explain to people that you are supposed to go to church, because that is just what you are supposed to do. It took falling away a bit for me to realize that I truly missed that *edification* in my life. I was missing services and the void was contributing to my depression. The longer I hid in those woods and made excuses for not being actively involved in worship, the further into depression I would fall.

The Chappells were always nearby with a solution of course and they invited me to visit the Ohatchee Church of Christ. I had several friends and even family who worshiped at that congregation and even knew great things about the Minister. A few "more conservative" friends were against me attending Ohatchee. According to one friend they were way too accepting of divorcees at Ohatchee. None of that mattered to me. I needed help and I reached out. My struggle with the Church of Christ has always been their overwhelming attitude that you must attend one specific congregation, because this one is not as sound as that one, etc. We are making strides, but my brethren and I have a long way to go if we hope to demonstrate love and acceptance of all people in *The Church*.

The second phase of change I needed to commit to was a move closer to my family and loved ones. I was able to shift some territory and responsibility at my job and I moved back into Calhoun County. This put me much closer to my mother and other relatives and now my new church family. I made drastic changes and it was necessary.

One of the toughest aspects of medical treatment for depression is the trial and error of the medication. There is no blood test that will let your doctor know exactly how to diagnose. There is no proven test or procedure to accurately prescribe the best cocktail of medication to deal with the symptoms of mental illness. Obviously, there is no cure. I find that medications work effectively for me in increments of three months. After about a quarter, I become immune and my physician and I will have to revisit the dosage or combinations. It can be frustrating with any medical crisis to have to live this way. You are almost never satisfied, so contentment feels unachievable.

Impulsive spending, sleepless nights, weight fluctuation, mood swings, sadness, thoughts of suicide all continued to haunt me in the months and year after Floyd Ray died. It wasn't long before I would say a final goodbye to my last grandparent. Edith Gowens declined quickly at the end of 2005. She spent the last couple of years in a home in Ragland, Alabama. Aunt Wormy and I would visit together along with my uncles, Gary and Glennis. I felt cheated that I really only had about eight good years with my paternal grandmother. We became close friends when my biological father died in 1997 and I truly enjoyed the time I was able to spend with her and the relationships it started for me with the rest of my Gowens family. I did my best to hide my depression from them also.

Death is common, right? Just as surely as you are born, you are going to die. We all endure this reality and we all have to hold on to the truth, life goes on. For those of us with faith, grief should be easier. We know there is an after life. We know with every fiber of our being that we will be reunited with our loved ones in Paradise. I will never be able to completely understand or explain how people deal with this common life occurrence, so differently. It's chemical. Everything emotional is chemical and we have to remember that. We have to be able to look to the Heavens and chant, "I believe, but Lord I am doing the best I can."

As time began to pass, I became more and more involved in the congregation at Ohatchee and my recovery began to progress. I found a sweet spot between medical assistance, faith-based therapy, and friends. I will always be an advocate for seeking medical attention for depression. Prescriptions can save lives, it's just not a perfect process and people need to understand the trial and error process. Any medication can yield symptoms that may make a patient feel worse than they did before, but you just have to keep trying until you find exactly what works with your own chemical imbalances.

I began a new commitment to my prayer life by journaling. Every day I would sit in a quiet place in my home or office and write a prayer letter to God. I write them just as I am speaking. I pour my heart out and ask for guidance. I confess sins and seek forgiveness. I am honest with God and I ask for what I need, whether it is financial, physical, emotional or spiritual.

I learned so many valuable lessons along the way and through this process of documentation I was better able to assist my doctors in the accurate diagnosis of Bipolar Disorder. Journaling is crucial in achieving an accurate diagnosis. Mental illnesses have so many similar symptoms and side effects. They share attributes and I can now fully understand how a medical professional could be deceived or mislead. When you are dealing with life a death, a patient must be completely honest. Journaling made it easier for me to do that. If a person decides to speak to a physician about their depression, it is truly important to document your feelings, symptoms, behavior, etc., leading up to the visit. Giving every ounce of information to a doctor will increase the chances of an accurate diagnosis and treatment plan.

I made a lot of mistakes when I first sought medical treatment. I spent a couple of years playing doctors against each other. I would visit a Psychiatrist for a while and if I didn't like what one said, I would choose another. I didn't give prescriptions ample time to work or develop in my system. I made all kinds of impulsive mistakes, but fortunately I was on the right track with my spirituality and God wouldn't turn His back on me. I felt a strong urge to return to my family medical doctor in Jacksonville where I had been a patient since the age of 13. Dr. Ingram knew most of my history with gastrointestinal problems, blood pressure, etc. He was not surprised when I confided in him about my depression. He read my journal and became extremely active in my recovery. He assisted me in reducing unnecessary meds and replacing them with more accurate doses for my condition. He is not a Psychiatrist, but as a medical doctor who treats many patients with mental illnesses, he is kind, knowledgeable and willing to do the research to help anyone. Dr. Ingram, his nurse Pam and their staff have played a major role in saving my life, from a medical perspective. Dr. Ingram is also a spiritual man and I believe God lead me to trust and depend on him.

Wayne Dunaway, my Minister at Ohatchee is one of those casual laid-back guys who has taken his role as a Shepherd to heart. It's totally his craft and I am a firm believer he was born to preach God's word and lead a flock. Wayne dove right into my life and struggles and encouraged me to share my journey with others. We shared the same philosophy about just how detrimental The Church can be to a person who struggles with depression. Judgment is the last thing a depressed individual needs to feel. I saw it too much growing up in an ultraconservative church. The idea that depression is caused by a lack of faith is ridiculous. It is certainly made worse if the person doesn't have hope or faith in something, but a faithful Christian can suffer from depression just like a non-believer. I think the recovery can be easier for a Christian if their Church is willing to help rather than hurt. I was blessed to find that help, support and guidance in Wayne and the Ohatchee Church of Christ.

I have dealt with depression and Bipolar Disorder since the age of five years old. I know all the ins and outs of sin and how that can affect my condition and I also know that I can be a faithful servant of God and still fall victim to my disease, it's chemical. God is part of my treatment plan, the most important part. If faith alone cured depression, mine would be gone. With Wayne's encouragement, I launched my first speaking tour on the topic of faith and depression, called "Faith Is A Factor."

While traveling to several congregations across the southeast to share my message, a regional health and wellness magazine asked me to publish my story. The following article appeared in Healthy Horizons Health and Wellness Magazine:

Faith Is A Factor

When I spoke publicly for the first time about my personal battle with depression and my advocacy for others with the same struggles, my mission was to remove the shameful stigma attached with the disease. I stood before two hundred or so of my brothers and sisters in Christ and poured my heart out about my deepest secrets. It was painful for my family and those who loved me to hear the thoughts I had actually entertained. The amount of support I received was astonishing, because I had always feared the worst. I spoke matter of fact about my rearing in the church and being taught that depression was a sign of weakness in faith. I disputed that teaching. I am going to stand before the same *group in another week or so, plus a few more, and I have decided to communicate the message that **faith is a factor**.*

Depression is not caused by a lack of faith, but certainly can lead to weakness in that area. In order to illustrate that point, I am going to have to make it personal. I certainly don't want to offend anyone with the intimate details, but when I started this mission to serve God, spread my testimony and perhaps save the lives of others, I conquered my fears of embarrassment. The people I have been fortunate to meet over the last four to five years on this journey share much of the same outlook as I do. Once again, we did not become depressed because we distrusted or had little faith in God; however, we have suffered moments of weak faith during our emotional cycles. I want to help others learn how to pull themselves out of the situation that causes weak faith and learn to become even stronger in their relationship with God.

Depression and Bipolar disorder is not something I woke up with one morning. It has been an illness I have dealt with my entire life; however, it went undiagnosed for many years, just as people often go undiagnosed for illnesses like Fibromyalgia, Diabetes, or Heart Disease. A mental illness is harder to diagnose because you can't exactly pinpoint it with a blood test, MRI, or regular office exam. It takes a lot of discussion, documenting symptoms and trial and error. It is proven that it can be hereditary. When my first significant adult manic episode occurred, I was twenty eight years old and a Youth Minister, Bible School Teacher and on the publishing team for a major Christian magazine. My career was at an all time high, I was financially stable and tithing more than I ever had before. My faith was strong publicly and privately. As the depression began to increase, every aspect of my life began to fall apart. I began to make impulsive and negative decisions with career, relationships and of course I began to distance myself from God. I did not blame God for my declining happiness and increasing stress, I just stopped going to Him in prayer for help and I started making excuses for skipping church services.

Over the course of the next few years I covered up episodes and deceived my family, friends and coworkers. I couldn't deceive God regardless of how hard I tried. When a man becomes a Christian, the Holy Spirit dwells within him and I believe that life gets harder when you turn away after obeying the Gospel rather than if you had never known God. He loves us so much that He will do whatever it takes to bring us home. Naturally, the more I lost faith, the harder it was to cope. As I reflect now, it occurs to me just how much of a factor faith is when dealing with depression. If I had reached out sooner, let me rephrase that, if I had reached up sooner to God, my actual path to better health could have been shorter and less rocky.

Throughout my life I have heard many preachers tell me they felt called to preach. Many women tell me they feel called to teach. My cousin Sherry has a beautiful soprano voice, and she tells me that she feels called to sing as part of her ministry. You never really understand the true meaning of what you are "called" to do until the passion is so strong in your heart that you know God put it there. I know without any doubt that God intends for me to remain an advocate for emotional wellness. He wants me to use my experiences, open mind, and talents to make a difference and shine for Him.

If you are affected by an emotional illness directly or indirectly by a loved one who suffers, whether you understand the disease or not, it can't be ignored. Depression can be a matter of life or death. Pray for yourselves and loved ones. Please share this blog and help me reach as many of God's children as possible. Faith is a factor. In my story it was the determining factor and saved my life.

CHAPTER EIGHTEEN

Friendship is a gift from God. I believe the people we encounter in our lives is divine intervention. While some relationships may appear to evolve through happenstance, others seem destined from the get go to result in life long camaraderie. My expertise in mental health lies within my own experience, where God has lead me to research and study, and through those I have met and shared stories. In my humble opinion, in order to win against depression it takes *God, Friends, and Medicine*. When depression creeps in, tell God, tell a friend, and tell your doctor.

With God's guidance, I have been able to surround myself with a wonderful support group. I look back on my school days at Pleasant Valley and that very difficult time of Junior High when I felt as though I had no friends, and I would never want to end up that way again. I am my happiest surrounded by loved ones, whether blood related, or simply given to me by the Father as a blessing.

After successfully launching two summer speaking tours, I also formed a support group at the Ohatchee Church with the help of Jean Chappell. Jean faced one of her hardest battles in life when she lost Brother C.E. A rare tumor formed in his Pituitary Gland and he was gone in a matter of months. C.E. was a rock to Jean, to me, his daughter Karen and so many others. I was the first person Jean had told in many years of her battle with depression, but along the way she became more confident and even helped me to lead support groups. She was instrumental in helping several other men and women seek help and therapy for their disease. C.E. Chappell was an outstanding Disciple in The Church, always looking out for the underdog and Jean carried his work right on. I have never met a more spiritually generous couple.

In the spring of 2010, I began feeling better than I had in years. The combination of God, friends and doctors truly had me on a great path. My friend Paul and I ventured out into the Caribbean on a Carnival Cruise to Cozumel, Mexico. I found some great stability in my recovery plan with my doctors, stayed very involved in the work at Ohatchee, and my career was going in a great new direction. Blessed with many friends, I really started to feel like I was headed toward a better quality of life. I always knew that I wanted to write and there was a natural talent and passion that went so well with public speaking. I became determined to tell my story and celebrate how God works in our lives to bring beauty, joy, and healing even in the darkest of times.

One of my favorite things about traveling on a cruise is the clarity one can find out on the open seas. There is nothing like sitting on the deck of a ship and watching a thunderstorm dance across the waves miles in the distance, or diving into crystal blue waters off the coast of Cozumel and feeling that coolness rush through your body, or maybe the star-filled nights on the top deck staring into the galaxy. I knew I was going to commit the rest of my life to being a writer, regardless if I had to flip hamburgers all day, mop floors, or push paperwork from one office to another. I was destined to be a writer and I knew my calling was to take the experience that God allowed me to survive and share it with the world in the hopes of saving one person, the way I had been saved. I think we all have a little bit of Narcissism in our blood. There's a certain sense of pride in recognizing that God has chosen you to share a message. A God-given talent can't be masked and to attempt to ignore it would be a disservice to ourselves and our Creator. Of course I want to be recognized. I certainly want to have my work acknowledged and would love to reach thousands of people who don't know God or what He has the ability to do for them. I would love to help thousands get on track with their lives and get their emotions under control by sharing these wonderful stories of Bertie Mae, my Alabama upbringing and the importance of family and faith. I also realize that in addition to accomplishing goals, writing is the best way to save my own life.

Depressed people will tell you that in their hearts they feel it is inevitable that one day they will take their own life. Not everyone sits around and thinks about it, plots it, or even wraps up the loose ends of their life. Depressed people will dwell on misery and lack of hope. It's what we do. For me, writing is accountability. Writing is essential therapy and a significant part of my treatment plan. I share everything I write with Sherilyn, Paul, Tracy, Michelle, and many others in my support system. My sense of pride for what I have written, or my twinge of narcissism has kept me alive in recent years, so I keep writing.

I followed up my 2010 cruise to Cozumel with a repeat in 2011. This time, Paul and I brought along four sweet lady friends with us. Tracy, Cindy, Angie, and Tonya joined us as we sailed again in the spring of 2011 to enjoy God's beauty. I find such great comfort in the lives of my friends. I am also blessed to have friends of all ages, creeds, race, and even religion. Dealing with my own personal demons have certainly helped me to become more open minded toward others. Judgment exists when we don't understand where other people are coming from. We fear the unknown. We have a natural tendency to put up barriers and protect ourselves from some way of life that we think is completely different from our own. Whether race, religion or sexuality is a distinction among people, we all still face many of the same obstacles.

I was completely ready for the summer of 2011 and prepared to launch another round of sermons and seminars on the topic of Christians and Depression. My editor at Healthy Horizons, Teresa Tims asked me to take part in a regional health fair and talk about my journey. I was honored and definitely prepared to share my story and the good news of recovery. The health fair was set for the end of summer after my speaking tour. On June 25 I was at my home in Alabama preparing for a sermon the next morning at the Ohatchee Church. Before going to bed that Saturday evening I saw a message on social media that interstate 20 was closed between Heflin and Oxford due to a traffic accident. As sick feeling began to churn in my stomach, but I shrugged it off and went to bed.

The startling sound of the telephone ringing at night is one of the most awful and cruel noises to pierce the ears. Immediately a person is riddled with confusion, worry, and panic. I answered my phone and immediately heard the worst sounds of my life, my mother's screams. Tony was dead. Killed in that accident on I-20. My stepbrother was gone. I was in shock and truly wanted to die right along with him.

The coming days were horrific. We were not able to see Tony's body and have what I would call an appropriate closure. The funeral director would not even allow me to place my hand in his casket and simply touch him. I just wanted to touch the body and know it was actually Tony. There is no explanation and no possible way of understanding when you lose a loved one in a tragic accident. It's not the same as losing someone to cancer. There is no chance to say goodbye. There is no time to prepare. I just couldn't grasp how God expected us to survive this. We needed him. My mother loved her stepson and she needed him because he represented my father so much. He was Floyd Ray's firstborn. Austin needed his uncle. He had me, but I wasn't enough. He needed Tony. My sister needed her eldest brother. He was the strong one. He was rational. He was comical. He was fun! I needed him!

Paul, Tracy, Cindy, Angie and Tonya surrounded me along with many other friends. Tracy moved right into my apartment and didn't leave unless Paul, Cindy or someone else was there to watch me. I have the most wonderful friends who step right in and take over when needed. Jean Chappell stood firm and ready to encourage me to keep going. She was prepared to take me to a doctor or hospital immediately. Tony's death was horrific and tragic, but I was so much more prepared than before. My friends were more prepared. They were like a well-oiled machine. I began to realize how God brought me to a more mature mindset as a Christian and how being on the right path of treatment for my Bipolar Disorder would help me to handle this tragedy so much better than I had years earlier.

Tony's biological mother asked me to speak at his funeral and so I did. I talked about the wonderful relationship I had with my brother. I truly believe that I was his best friend after we became adults. He was a steadying force to me. I didn't try any crazy stuff with him, he just didn't put up with it. He saw me as a super intelligent and successful guy and Tony never allowed me to see myself any differently.

Tony R. Goodwin, my beloved big brother. He went home too
soon, but I know we'll be reunited in Paradise one day.

Wayne Dunaway encouraged me to get back behind the podium and
complete my commitments to speak. He didn't want to see me regress
back into a terrible state of depression. Speaking publicly again was
very difficult for me because I knew there was no way to do it without
acknowledging Tony's untimely death and how it had affected my
emotions. I spent the rest of the summer working hard and pretending
all was fine during the day, but at night in the dark, I battled those
horrible demons.

Jean offered her condo in Fairhope as a resource for an emotional
retreat. Fairhope is a jewel of a town on Mobile Bay. My close circle of
friends and I headed down for a long weekend over Labor Day. Tony's
birthday fell on the Sunday we were there and I barely found the energy
to climb out of bed. I had to be able to take my own advice and deal
with whatever came at me. Even though I was struggling, I couldn't
be a hypocrite. I had to do the work and get back on my feet. Death is
very fair it happens to all of us. It's the time and the method of death
that we have such an incredible problem with. We are never prepared
when a loved one's time is up and we never like the method. Depressed
people have a more difficult time *moving on* or coping with grief, even
those of us who have faith.

Grief has only two directions to go, it can get better or it can get worse. After Bertie Mae's death my grief got worse. It grew to this bottomless dark pit where all I could see around me was darkness and despair. I didn't have the energy to raise an arm or leg at times. It developed into a terrible cycle of depression that nearly cost me my own life. After Dad and then Tony's deaths I didn't seem to grieve as long. I don't think we become immune or cold to loss of life, I think it is part of our emotional maturity. I didn't love my Dad or Brother any different than I loved Bertie Mae. Maybe I just clung to her more. I also feel that the anxiety and lamenting about her death as a young boy made it so much worse when it finally happened. I think parents or guardians of children who have too much anxiety or worry truly have to pay attention and seek help for this kind of behavior because it can ruin a childhood and set them up for a tumultuous emotional life as an adult.

The larger the family, the more likely we are to experience frequency of grief. If ten people are in a family, one person is going to suffer grief for at least nine times. When someone dies, we don't know what to say or do. We pray for God to comfort and we prepare food and try and give as much support as we can. This is the only humanly possible thing a person can do for one another. Death is natural and so is grief. Depression occurs when that grief lasts and lingers and prevents a person from living a normal life. I'll always miss my brother and other family members who died so suddenly, but I am grateful to God for allowing me to arrive at a place where I am better equipped to deal with my grief. God's comfort and mercy truly shows itself when our ability to understand or cope with life comes to a halt.

CHAPTER NINETEEN

I don't mind getting older. I actually really had a great time turning the big 4-0. I have always been an old soul and enjoyed being around people twice my age. There is a great deal of wisdom and perspective that comes with age. I enjoy those ah-ha moments of life where you just kind of smile to yourself and whisper, "now I get it."

My best friends put together an outstanding bash for me in the spring of 2012. My sweet friend Michelle and her husband flew all the way to Alabama from Seattle to surprise me. Michelle and I met on a website especially for people with mental health issues. We began emailing each other back and forth sharing our struggles, joys, ups and downs, and we formed a great bond. I have traveled to see her and she has been to Alabama on multiple occasions. It was a great feeling to walk into my party and see Kevin and Michelle sitting there. My close cousins, coworkers and dearest friends showered me with love and I knew this next decade was going to be the best.

I preached the next day at our Church service and then Mom served over a hundred of our closest friends chicken and dumplings. I had a wonderful celebration and it was a great way to mark a new chapter in life and celebrate some of my writing accomplishments and advancements. I believe that God is right there beside me making things happen and clearing the way for me to fulfill a destiny cultivated just for me. When my mind forces me into one of those dark places where hope becomes slippery, I remember He is there ready to catch me just in case I lose my grip.

As a little boy I sat between Bertie Mae and Ms. Pearl Dobbs during worship service. As a forty-year old man, I sat between Jean Chappell and our dear friend Nell McElroy. Nell and Jean were like sisters and had both been through breast cancer and the loss of their spouses. Nell is one of those demure ladies possessing all the attributes of a Southern Belle. Nell loves everyone unconditionally and I have enjoyed laying my head on her shoulder and talking for hours, holding her hand in church, and praying together over wonderful meals in her home. Nell and Jean were absolute best friends. Both widowed, they shopped together, teased each other about potential male suitors, and doted on me as if I was their own son.

Jean's health began to decline the summer of 2012. Jean really never got over losing C.E. She made it clear to everyone in her life, especially daughter Karen and close friends Nell and I that she was ready to be with him in Paradise. Jean developed COPD, began to weaken, and become hospitalized.

Jean spent time recovering in our local rehabilitation facility after losing the ability to walk and she was not happy. She wanted to be home or really anywhere besides where she was. She was determined to break out of this place. Karen, Nell and I tried desperately to calm her and we rotated our visits so that she didn't experience a lot of alone time. One night she decided it was all she could take. She got down in the floor, dialed 9-1-1 on her cell phone and asked the paramedics to come to the rehab facility and pick her up. The nurses were astonished when the ambulance showed up to collect a patient who called from her own room. Of course she told them she had fallen, but later she whispered in my ear that "there was more than one way to skin a cat." Even at the end of her life, Jean had humor and charisma and just made me feel wonderful about who I am. She was in control and she meant it.

Jean's health declined in the coming weeks and we really didn't know what was in store, but her mind remained sharp. I truly believe that she bargained with God. I think she was so determined to join C.E. in Heaven. She lived a great Christian life and it was almost as if she dialed God up on her cell phone and said, "come get me or else!"

I was able to spend all day on Saturday with her. She sat next to me on her couch at home and could barely hold her head up. I had a flashback to the time she took me to the Psychiatrist. She placed a pillow in the back seat of her car, then on her lap and motioned for me to lay down. She told me the pillow was there because "I thought you might need it." That Saturday, I placed a pillow on my lap sitting next to Jean on the sofa, she laid down, and rested her head in my lap. I sat there and stroked her hair for what seemed like hours. *Jean knew I needed that too.* She knew that I needed a sweet way to say goodbye to my friend. My rescuer. Jean Chappell saved my life years earlier and here I was on this day being given this beautiful opportunity by God to thank her one last time. I stayed with her until Sunday morning and one day later she hopped over the pearly gates and ran into the arms of C.E. Chappell, the love of her life.

If we are lucky enough to have memories, we have everything! Memories are where we store life's most important moments and lessons. I know it sounds kind of cliché' to say that we carry our loved ones with us in our hearts, but that is probably the most eloquent way to say it. Have you ever sat and thought about how God utilized others to shape who you are? The sum total of who we are is where we have been and who we have known. Someone somewhere influences every decision that we make, positive or negative.

Human life is so important. Suicide is selfish and I say this as a person who has plotted and tried. I don't believe it is ever the only answer, nor do I believe it is ever *the best* answer. I do understand how people get to that place. I ache for those of us who do. I pray that God will always allow someone to intervene. As a person who suffers from depression, I have to stay accountable. I have to remain in a position to see how others are trying to help me and allow them to do so.

I think about Jean often. I would be doing a terrible disservice to her life and her legacy if I commit suicide. Jean did many things for many people, but if I truly appreciate the kind of friend she was to me, I have to go the distance. I feel the same about Bertie Mae. I want to give her a voice long after she is gone. She was a simple southern lady who touched many lives with her candor, humility, and love. It's my job to keep those memories at the forefront and see if I can be the difference to someone else like those ladies were to me. Yes, I admit that suicide is selfish and it is a cruel way to leave your family and loved ones. We have to open those memories like a vault and sift through the old times and apply the lessons. We have to appreciate how God places instrumental people in our path at significant times. We make wrong turns in life and start heading down unfamiliar and dangerous roads, but friends are often the pass-thru in the median. Friends are our perfect path to turn around and get back on the right road.

CHAPTER TWENTY

Living with Bipolar Disorder has been quite a journey for me to say the least. I am not grateful for the disease, but I am thankful for the clarity and better understanding that I have been able to achieve through spiritual study, medical advancements and information made available through technology. Just like any other ailment, a mental illness needs to be researched, treated professionally, and managed as the chronic illness it is. Depression has been viewed differently than other illnesses and that is why I wrote this book. Shame on us if we allow mental illness to stay an embarrassment or taboo in society and in *The Church*. I refuse to loosely use terms like "crazy" or "insane" to describe someone who deals with emotions differently than others. We all learn as we get older there is no clear definition of normal. Advertisements/Movies/TV Shows give us a glimpse of what most would call normal based on what a demographic spends the most money and for what brand. Normal is made up of a group of branded clothes, shoes, movies, music, cars, and you name it...all material things. Normal has nothing to do with spirituality, intelligence, or love. Sometimes I wonder if normal is really just being abnormal?

I set out to change the world a little bit. Maybe just the world that I live in, but hey if Rob Goodwin can stand up and let everyone know that he struggles with thoughts of hopelessness, suicide, and grief, but is still able to be successful in life, then maybe others will feel they can too. What I have gained in abundance on this journey of self-discovery and public acknowledgement of my battle is compassion. I have found that human beings are a lot more compassionate than we give them credit for. Our world was designed by a perfect Higher Being we call God. He placed us on this earth to support and love one another and not to judge.

We demonstrated for God right away that humans are nowhere near perfect. We are sinful and disgusting at times. We abandon one another, we cheat, lie, steal, kill, and do whatever it takes to elevate ourselves. This was not God's vision for the world, but it happened nonetheless. Along the way God said, "well I will just show you what unconditional love is." He sent Jesus to live the life we are not capable of living, to die the death we are not capable of dying, and to win the battle against sin we are not capable of winning. It has all been done for us.

The least we can do is support one another and appreciate our individual struggles. We can offer support without blame, encouragement without condemnation, and love without condition. The Church has a long way to go to be where it needs to be, but we are making strides. As Christians, we have to be the example we want people to see in our communities. *When you look at the world and you see all of things wrong with it, decide what needs to be different and change that about yourself first.*

When I realized that I could use my voice to save my own life from the grips of depression, I realized that very thing holding me back was feeling that I would never be good enough or deserve to be saved. None of us are independently worthy of redemption, but because Jesus has already paid the price, we don't have to be worthy. His blood makes us worthy.

Occasionally I encounter non-believers who suffer from depression. I don't believe they are suffering because they are non-believers because it is entirely chemical, but I do think the road to recovery has to be paved with faith and determination. You must have faith in something otherwise where is your hope grounded? God has not forsaken us and no matter how dark the hour becomes or how intense our struggle, God is omnipresent.

Thirty years have gone by since I left that small country school called Roy Webb. I still long for it at times and the security that I felt behind those walls. I miss the faces of the people who helped me to lose my worries during long school days. I think about how we played such a role in each other's rearing. We all had a hand in cultivating who one another would become.

I decided that I wanted to see this group again. My good friends Deborah and Jason own the house right across the street from the school building. Roy Webb reopened its doors as a special school for the handicapped called The Learning Tree. Deb and Jason were definitely up for a class reunion so we reached out to everyone we could find and planned a big cookout and thirty year reunion. A good old-fashioned cook out at Roy Webb was something we all needed and could bring our lives full circle. In the fall of 2013 we gathered together once again on the Roy Webb Road. We shared hugs and great memories. We rekindled old friendships and promised to support one another for the rest of our lives. The great thing about Roy Webb is that all of these years later we were able to reach 90% of our classmates. Although not everyone was able to attend, we had a good crowd and the day was beautiful.

Chris Dempsey arranged a surprise for us. The Learning Tree allowed us to all tour the old school building. As we walked across those old shiny hard wood floors, gazing down the slender dark hallways that once seemed so large and overpowering, I couldn't help but become teary-eyed. This is my vault. This is where my memories are stored and they have shaped my life in such a way that I can't thank this school, this community and these people enough. I love them all as if they were my siblings.

A few of my classmates from Roy Webb at our
2013 reunion. What a blessing!

Recently I made a trip to Hanceville, Alabama located in Cullman County just about an hour and half northwest of my home in Jacksonville. My Uncle Glennis and Aunt Dean live on a farm there. Over the years I have grown even closer to the Gowens family and we have done all we can to make up for lost time. Uncle Glen, the rest of the family and I were sitting on his back porch when he told me that he wanted to share a story with me. Many years ago he was back home visiting his mother Edith Gowens and my biological father, Bob came for a visit as well. The two brothers strolled around the property and my Dad pulled out a knife. It was a beautiful old pocketknife used for hunting. He asked his older brother to buy the knife for $5, no doubt to buy some cigarettes or gas. Uncle Glen obliged, as he was an avid knife collector. He pulled this beautiful old knife from his pocket and placed it in my hand. "It's yours now, Rob" he told me. I was very moved and thanked him for the generosity. Over the years I have collected a few things here and there that belonged to Bob. I was pleased to get another.

My mother and her sisters Myrtle and Emily are getting older now. Their brothers have all passed on as well as their first husbands. They work together keeping the family graves clean and decorated. I recently visited Bertie Mae's grave. I don't go very often because I know she is not there, she is in Paradise waiting for me. She is also in my dreams and beside me when I need her, but it's a family tradition to visit the graves, so I went. The Cochran family cemetery is nestled on a small hill surrounded by woods just off Alabama highway 21 where they raised cotton for so many years. The wind rushes through the trees and makes the most peaceful noise. You can't help but find serenity when you visit this old gravesite.

My mother and her two sisters visiting their "old home place" in 2008. Emily Hill-Sharpton, Myrtle Lane and Ona Lee Goodwin

I sat on the cinderblock wall surrounding the graves of Bertie Mae, Luther and JD Cochran. I stared at the name carved in the stone, Bertie Mae. I couldn't help but wonder if this modern world would ever know what a magnificent woman she was and how much good she did for the Kingdom. She has been gone from this life for more than ten years, but what is important is that I know. I know what kind of woman she was and I experienced it. I am alive today because of the seeds she planted and the special love and attention she gave to me. I will know and I will always remember.

Today I am sitting on my back deck enjoying the beautiful sunshine and clear blue skies. If I look to the left from my deck there is a beautiful flat piece of land and the grass underneath is as green as I would imagine it being in the hills of Ireland. I know what would be perfect for that little corner of my world, my own little piece of therapy. I think I will build it right now….yes, that's where I will put my "porch swing."

EPILOGUE

There are three commitments I believe we have to make in order to conquer emotional issues. The first is to **pray about it.** Take everything to God in prayer. I used to make excuses and say that I just hurt too much to pray. I also felt that I was not worthy of God's help because my faith seemed to be slipping. What I had to realize is that God wants me to turn to Him in my hour of need. As a Christian, I finally conformed. There is nothing in life I can accomplish or even want to accomplish that I don't take to him first. I am one of those guys who tries to track everything I do, so I write it down. I have a daily prayer journal and I write down my feelings, desires, needs, etc. God is the first person I go to before my best friend, family, etc.

The second commitment is **talk about it.** I will never make the mistake again of bottling my feelings up inside. Hiding from your problems will only make them worse. True friends are there to listen even if they can't do anything to help you. Once I have told my thoughts to God, I can tell them to anyone. I am no longer ashamed to say that I can't always control my emotions. I refuse to allow society to dictate how I live my life. I encourage anyone who suffers from depression or related illnesses to confide in your friends and family. It assigns accountability to yourself for your own actions and makes you accountable to others. It can keep you alive. In addition to talking, you will find yourself actually listening. In the emotional wellness workshop at church we each were able to gain insight on handling certain situations and realize that we were not alone.

The final commitment is **be about it,** which means do something! Don't be idle. Be about it. Get out and make something happen. Go to the doctor. Get some exercise. Read about your condition online and find out what your options are. Most people find medication to be helpful. The most important thing to remember about taking medication for depression or other mental illnesses is that we are all different. What works for someone else's chemical imbalance may not work the same for yours. Also, there is a need for trial and error. Our bodies are always changing and if one medication does not work, it's very possible that another one will. You have to take control just as if it were any other physical illness. You must manage it exactly the same. Please do not be sedentary when dealing with mental illness. Mental illness is no respecter of persons. It can affect anyone, regardless of age, race, gender, etc.

Philippians 2:2 says, "Agree with each other. Love each other. Be deep spiritual friends." God instructs us to reach out to one another in an effort to prepare us for eternal love and eternal life. We need to make every effort to be great friends with one another. Small thoughtful acts of kindness are more important than grand gestures. Friendship is built on equality and caring for one another. I encourage everyone to cultivate circles of friends to walk with you along this journey of life. Love to you all!

In the south cousins are more like siblings, in my family Bertie Mae created that bond between us that will never be broken.

Through my treatment plan for Bipolar Disorder, I met another patient in an online support group. Michelle Moe is from Seattle and has become one of my closest friends and strongest members of my support team.

My sisters, Sherry, Rhonda, and Becky all showed up to celebrate my 40th birthday bash. I know the four of us will grow old together!

Life is good. Paul, Tonya, Angie and I were blessed with a beautiful vacation to the Keys in 2012. I am embracing life and thankful to be a child of God.